IMAGES OF ASIA

Chinese Painting

Titles in the series

At the Chinese Table
T. C. LAI

Balinese Paintings (2nd ed.)
A. A. M. DJELANTIK

Bamboo and Rattan:
Traditional Use and Beliefs
JACQUELINE M. PIPER

The Birds of Java and Bali
DEREK HOLMES and
STEPHEN NASH

The Birds of Sumatra and Kalimantan
DEREK HOLMES and
STEPHEN NASH

Borobudur (2nd ed.)
JACQUES DUMARÇAY

The Chinese House: Craft, Symbol, and the Folk Tradition
RONALD G. KNAPP

Chinese Jade
JOAN HARTMAN-GOLDSMITH

Chinese Painting
T. C. LAI

Early Maps of South-East Asia (2nd ed.)
R. T. FELL

Folk Pottery in South-East Asia
DAWN F. ROONEY

Fruits of South-East Asia: Facts and Folklore
JACQUELINE M. PIPER

A Garden of Eden: Plant Life in South-East Asia
WENDY VEEVERS-CARTER

The House in South-East Asia
JACQUES DUMARÇAY

Images of the Buddha in Thailand
DOROTHY H. FICKLE

Indonesian Batik: Processes, Patterns and Places
SYLVIA FRASER-LU

Japanese Cinema: An Introduction
DONALD RICHIE

The Kris: Mystic Weapon of the Malay World (2nd ed.)
EDWARD FREY

Life in the Javanese Kraton
AART VAN BEEK

Macau
CESAR GUILLEN-NUÑEZ

Mammals of South-East Asia (2nd ed.)
EARL OF CRANBROOK

Mandarin Squares: Mandarins and their Insignia
VALERY M. GARRETT

The Ming Tombs
ANN PALUDAN

Musical Instruments of South-East Asia
ERIC TAYLOR

Old Bangkok
MICHAEL SMITHIES

Old Manila
RAMÓN MA. ZARAGOZA

Old Penang
SARNIA HAYES HOYT

Old Singapore
MAYA JAYAPAL

Sarawak Crafts: Methods, Materials, and Motifs
HEIDI MUNAN

Silverware of South-East Asia
SYLVIA FRASER-LU

Songbirds in Singapore: The Growth of a Pastime
LESLEY LAYTON

Traditional Chinese Clothing in Hong Kong and South China 1480–1980
VALERY M. GARRETT

Series Editors, China Titles:
NIGEL CAMERON, SYLVIA FRASER-LU

Chinese Painting

T. C. LAI

HONG KONG
OXFORD UNIVERSITY PRESS
OXFORD NEW YORK
1992

Oxford University Press

Oxford New York Toronto
Petaling Jaya Singapore Hong Kong Tokyo
Delhi Bombay Calcutta Madras Karachi
Nairobi Dar es Salaam Cape Town
Melbourne Auckland

and associated companies in
Berlin Ibadan

First published 1992
Published in the United States
by Oxford University Press, Inc., New York
ISBN 0-19-585427-6

Library of Congress Cataloging-in-Publication Data

Lai, T.C.
Chinese Painting / T.C. Lai.
p. cm. — (Images of Asia)
Includes bibliographical references and index.
ISBN 0-19-585427-6
1.Painting, Chinese. I. Title. II. Series.
ND1040.L33 1992
759.951—dc20
92–4451
CIP

British Library Cataloguing in Publication Data available

Printed in Hong Kong
Published by Oxford University Press, Warwick House, Hong Kong

Preface

In this book I attempt to show, by means of carefully chosen examples, what Chinese painting is all about. I do this without delving too far into the academic background of each painting or taking the reader on an exhaustive tour through the maze of Chinese history. By avoiding works that are laden with Western influences, I have been left free to focus on the central issue: the Chineseness of Chinese painting.

It is this many-sided quality that has perplexed viewers, Westerners and Asians alike. My book sets out to show that an understanding of it is essential to pleasurable appreciation.

Contents

1

What Makes a Painting 'Chinese'?

ANYONE looking at Chinese painting for the first time, particularly if they are unacquainted with things Chinese or Asian, may well find that the art that confronts them is strange or bewildering. Even people brought up in the East complain that Chinese landscape painting defies space, disregards light and colour, and is cluttered with literary sayings and seals. I have heard comments from close acquaintances that the subject material in Chinese painting doesn't seem to matter at all, being merely a pretext for the artist to construct a kind of pictorial and calligraphic morse code, the better to convey philosophical or poetic thoughts to fellow *cognoscenti*. The implication that Chinese artists are an exclusive élite, sending each other beautiful messages, has not endeared their work to the general viewer.

However, as in all matters of art, one has to consider the intention of the artist, just as much as the immediate impressions of his or her technique, in order to remove prejudice from the eye. The conventions, aesthetic assumptions and above all, the brush-and-ink basis of Chinese painting, must be considered before the viewer can absorb what may turn out to be a very pleasurable aesthetic and emotional experience. Understanding the painting's background is essential if one is to see more than a few stylized trees, hills, and figures, interspersed with indecipherable cryptograms and strange markings.

In technical terms, the most distinctive feature of many Chinese paintings is the presence of words. These literary inscriptions may be simply a dedication followed by the painter's name or perhaps the time and place of the painting's execution; they may be a poem or a description of the picture; they may even be concerned with the techniques used in painting the picture. The size of the inscription varies from one vertical line to a dense cluster filling one side of the painting. They may be written by the painter himself, or they may be the words of a fellow-painter, a collector or a connoisseur who has chosen to add something special. Along with the one or more red seals of the painter or his friends, they comprise the literary context of the painting.

This context has always been important because of the relationship of Chinese painting with calligraphy. Inkstone and brush have traditionally been used for both painting and writing, and both have required similar techniques. Successful execution of the type-forms and other elements of a Chinese landscape painting have depended on fine brushwork and a command of the art of calligraphy, which in turn presupposes literary proficiency. Evidence of skill with the brush remained for centuries the primary criterion by which a painting's merits were judged. In modern times, when the brush has for all practical purposes been replaced by other types of writing instruments, the number of people who can appreciate good brushwork, much less produce it themselves, has greatly declined.

Most Chinese paintings are done on white, highly absorbent paper, called *hsüan* or 'rice paper'. A sized variety is used if a less absorbent surface is required. A very sensitive brush is needed to paint on this absorbent paper; it may be made up of the hair of a ram, rabbit, wolf or some other animal. Its tip consists of long springy hairs and at the base of this core is a layer of considerably shorter hairs, flanked again by strands of longer hair that act as a reservoir for the ink. A Chinese painting is often in black and white only, using ink and water in a way that creates many gradations of tone that

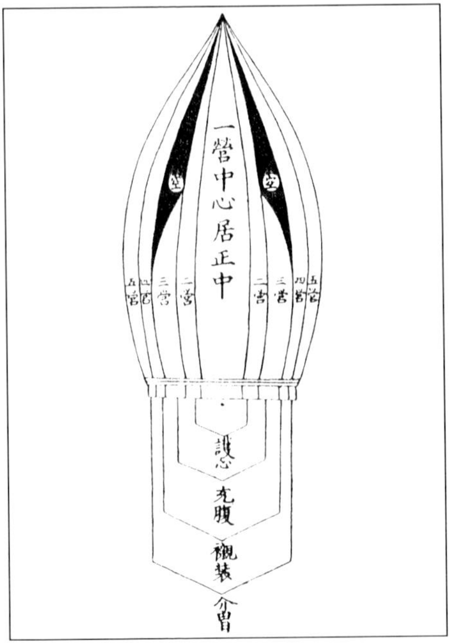

Brush tip
The picture shows the cross-section of a brush tip with five layers of hair of different length. The hollow space (black) is the ink reservoir. Each time the brush is dipped in ink, the point spreads out, absorbing the ink and allowing the fluid to enter the hollow space. When the brush is lifted up, the hairs at the tip close again and a quantity of ink is retained in the reservoir inside.

can be enjoyed for their own sake, but that sometimes create semblances of shading. In other words, although light and shade may appear to be there, the sources of light are often multi-directional and confused. By tradition, colour is sparingly applied, and many landscape paintings are lightly shaded with indigo or reddish-brown but little else.

However, to the viewer unaccustomed to Chinese painting, the biggest surprise may not be the absence of bright colour but the pictorial perspective. Distant objects may be depicted larger than nearer ones; the far side of a table may be longer than the nearer side. This is not so much due to the absence of perspective but, as we shall see, to the variety of perspectives. In turn, this is connected to the lack of any conscious attempt to indicate the source of light. Comparative light and shade may be indicated by gradation in ink tones and by the relative pressure of the brush, resulting in a greater or lesser mass of individual strokes, but there seems to be no precise point in Chinese painting from which the landscape is being observed. Perspective is not the primary concern of the artist.

One has to remember the conditions under which a painting is prepared. Since paper or silk becomes wrinkled and sometimes bubbly upon the application of water and ink, a Chinese painting at the untreated stage is not really ready for viewing. It has to be backed or mounted to remove the wrinkles and other blemishes on the surface. Only the finished product — a mounted scroll, album leaf, or whatever — can display the beauty of the painting.

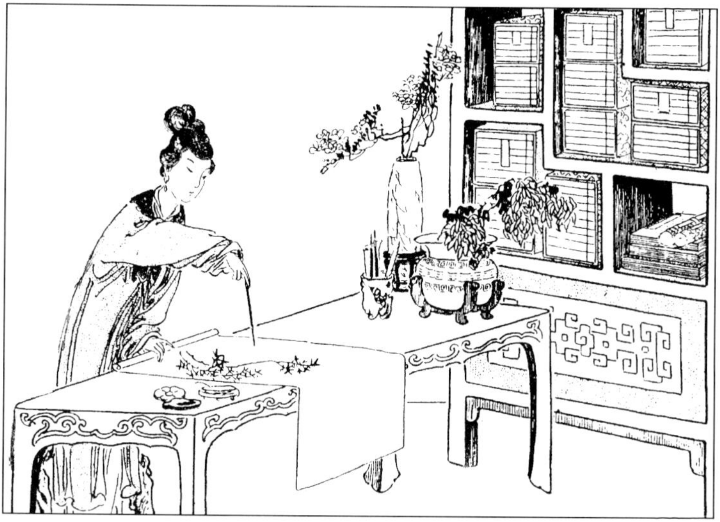

Woodblock print of a lady painting a bamboo
Note the inkstone, the flat porcelain dish with five compartments, the round water container with dispensing spoon, and the bookcase with books lying flat on the shelves. The brush is held vertically for maximum freedom of manoeuvre.

Chinese painters, whether amateur or professional, think of themselves as specializing in certain genres, although some are endowed with enough versatility to be proficient in all. Teachers of painting share this tendency to compartmentalize, preferring their students to study each genre at different times. Viewers too, regard painters in the context of their specialities, classifying them as landscapists, flower-and-bird painters, and so on. Unless they are particularly gifted, painters specialize because of the complexity of the brush techniques (for example, the expressive lines and type-forms) involved in executing a painting according to a genre's traditional format.

It is revealing to observe a connoisseur in front of a Chinese painting. If a casual glance has convinced the viewer that it deserves a second look, he or she will get closer and try to scrutinize the brushwork and inkwork — the quality of lines and dots, the quality of ink tonality. A masterpiece and copies of a masterpiece may look identical from a distance, but upon closer examination the finer details will begin to emerge, distinguishing the superior work from the ordinary. Lines and dots of a higher order produce work with finer 'touches'. These subtle qualities are much insisted on in Chinese painting.

In the following chapters, each of the qualities are considered in turn, beginning with their treatment in Chinese aesthetic thought.

2

Chinese Thought on Painting and Its Aesthetics

IN any culture, the philosophy and aesthetic background of art is likely to be a matter of discussion and often confused debate. In the history of Chinese aesthetic thought, it is difficult to find any two texts that entirely agree on viewpoint or interpretation, and indeed the terms of the debate themselves are often ambiguous or difficult to apply in specific cases.

It was not until the 5th century AD that any important body of thinking on Chinese literary and visual art is known to have developed. At that time, Liu Hsieh (active circa AD 460-530) wrote the revealingly titled *Literary Mind and the Carving of Dragons*, Chung Yung wrote his *Poetics*, and Hsieh Ho wrote *Critiques on Old Paintings*. The latter contains the much-quoted 'Six Elements of Painting', which have since become the cornerstones of Chinese painting theory. In brief, they say a painting should:

(a) Have a life of its own, be vibrant and resonant.
(b) Have good brushwork that gives it a sound structure.
(c) Bear some likeness to the nature of the subject.
(d) Have hues that answer the need of the situation.
(e) Have a well thought-out composition.
(f) Inherit the best of tradition through learning from it.

Ching Hao (AD 901–60), who lived during the Five Dynasties period, had clearly learnt from the tradition of Hsieh Ho when he wrote down his six elements of painting. These had a great influence on later artists, and indeed on later thinking about art. His first element was *chi* or 'air', which has no precise aesethetic equivalent in English but can be loosely translated to mean the life-force in a painting, created by the brush at the bidding of the artist's mind. His second element was *yun*, meaning a certain elegance and grace. The combination of *chi* and *yun* creates what Ching Hao defined as a 'lively vibrancy'. The third element was *szu*, meaning the conceptualization or the process by which objective reality is either included or excluded in order to arrive at a final image. His fourth element was *ching* or the process of 'imaging to find certain truths', giving a philosophical aim to the whole process. Fifthly, *bi* meant skilful manipulation of the brush to give life and movement to a painting. Lastly — and perhaps the most significant in terms of the difference between Western and Chinese approaches to painting — *mo*, meaning ink or ink tonality, depth and shade, that which adds further elegance to a work of art.

The pre-eminence of brushstrokes in the aesthetics of Chinese painting has its origins in Chinese calligraphy. During the first six centuries AD, calligraphic brush strokes were the dominant means of expression in Chinese painting, so much so that any means of painting other than with brushwork was frowned upon. As Chang Yan Yuan (c. AD 815–75) said in his book *Famous Paintings Through the Dynasties*:

> The ancients had not perfected the art of painting clouds. One way of creating clouds in a painting was this: first wet the surface of the silk, then sprinkle fine white powder over it while gently blowing on it. This was called 'blowing clouds', a natural way of creating clouds and a clever one too. But no trace of the brush is apparent and the result should not be called painting.

Modern Chinese painters are more open to the use of innovative tools and materials, but Chang's statement continues to be regarded by many scholars and artists as a self-evident truth. After all, Chinese scholars have always been by definition good calligraphers, that is, skilful handlers of the brush, and this proficiency has given them natural access to the world of painting. 'Brush' and 'ink' have been the key words in Chinese painting, both in the teaching and appreciation of it, ever since the time when people began to use the medium. Although it is still not commonly understood, full appreciation of a Chinese painting depends a great deal on the viewer's sensitivity to the movement of the brush, as represented by the strokes it makes. He or she may follow the brush as it progresses, dotting, flicking, sweeping, turning, poised to dart or plunging downwards. The pleasure lies in observing the dexterity and complexity of the painter's brushwork. This expressive skill, arguably unique to Chinese art, requires immense practise. As Tang Dei (1673–1752) wrote:

> Morning and evening one fondly takes up the brush, then tries to paint a dry branch, or some many-veined leaves or stones—like a calligrapher copying from a model—trying to capture the spirit of trees or stones. Arduous is the way to brush-control. When one finally finds the way, the mind and hand collaborate naturally.

The painting then is an intellectual as well as a technical challenge, and in this sense both good brushwork and ink tonality are vital to the artist. As Wang Yuan Chi (1642–1715), one of the famous 'Four Wangs', put it:

> One resorts to colour only when brush-and-ink is inadequate or when one wants to emphasize certain parts in spite of the already good brush-and-ink work. Nowadays, people do not understand the function of colour, allowing brush-and-ink and colour to lie

side by side in a painting, like strange bedfellows, and with disastrous results.

This predisposition towards brush-and-ink has continued into modern times. As the late Chang Da-Chien (1889–1983) said:

> In Chinese painting, light and colour are often separately used; the former is avoided whenever possible. Light and and shade are suggested by lines, their rise and fall, their twisting and turning...The ancient artists decided that 'shade' would destroy the aesthetic integrity of a painting, and preferred the use of colour to reinforce the effects made by lines.

One of the results of this is that the uninitiated often consider Chinese painting to have no sense of perspective. However, continues Chang Da-Chien, perspective in Chinese painting is not necessarily absent, merely different. It is taken from all directions instead of a single focal point. He suggests that Li Cheng's way of depicting Chinese pavilions is a good example. Li Cheng's contemporaries often complained that he painted pavilions showing the top of the roof together with parts under the eaves, which of course is not visually possible. But Chang Da-Chien observed that painting is concerned with beauty and art, and not necessarily objective reality. He did not see anything wrong with a painter depicting a bird's-eye view of the roof-top, and a worm's-eye view of the eaves simultaneously. After all, it would be a pity not to capture the beauty of both, the pride of Chinese architecture.

In this sense the pre-eminence of water and ink in the art of painting is closely related, as Wang Wei (AD 699–759) remarked, to Hsieh Ho's fifth element, that is, to the well thought-out composition, the visualization or conception that should precede the execution.

In this, as in many other aspects of Chinese culture, there is a tension between spontaneity and intellectual preparation, between subjective expression and objective form. Although brush-and-ink is the main technical concern of the traditional Chinese painter, a painting's success has also been judged on how far his technique has allowed the artist to express his thoughts and feelings. This in turn raises the question of inspiration.

Some of the qualities the Chinese connoisseur values most in a painting are spontaneity, naturalness and a grand sense of abandon. In Chapter 7 of his famous book, the philosopher Chuang Tzu (fl. c. 300 BC) tells a story about the Prince of Sung, who wanted a painting done for a special purpose. He had all the artists in the land summoned to his court, and they all came, anxious for the job–except one, who was found far removed from the crowd in a corner, his top robes casually loosened and his chest bared, looking quite unconcerned. When this was reported to the prince, he immediately said, 'That is the right man for the job.' Since then, 'baring one's chest' has become a standard phrase to describe that quality in a painting that successfully reflects the artist's breadth of vision, power and aloofness.

Contrary to the pedantry associated with calligraphic perfection and literary nicety, Chuang Tzu's story reveals the poetic strain in Chinese painting. Painting is a creative activity. As Ni Tsan (1301–74) commented on one of his paintings:

> My bamboos are a vehicle through which I try to release the hidden feelings in my heart. Who cares whether they look like real bamboo or not, whether the leaves are dense or sparse, or whether the branches are perpendicular or slanting?

An earlier poet and calligrapher, Su Shih (1039–1100) made a similar comment:

To say that painting should look like real life
Is to babble like ignorant children;
To want to write poetry but insist on a certain form
Is to reveal a non-poetic disposition.
Poëtry and painting are one and the same thing:
The product of natural gift and freshness of vision.

Su's comment on the art of Wang Wei, the Tang Dynasty poet, is equally applicable: 'There is poetry in his painting and painting in his poetry.'

The question of 'likeness and unlikeness' continued to exercise Chinese painters. Huang Bin-hong (1864–1955) had this to say on the subject:

There are three types of painting. Firstly, paintings that achieve verisimilitude; the painter may be popular for this, but there is no intrinsic worth. Secondly, paintings that do not look like things in life at all; the painters concerned may pretend they are trying only to capture the spirit, but they are bogus painters. Lastly, paintings that look unlike life but are absolutely life-like; these are real paintings.

But what about capturing the spirit? The combination of intense preparation, perfect technical command and a certain emotional readiness is perhaps best caught in this extract from Kuo Ju-Hsu's *Essay on Landscape Painting*, which describes how his father prepared for a painting session:

On a day when he intended to paint, he would find himself seated or standing by a bright window, his desk having been made tidy and clean; he would burn incense after getting ready a good brush and ink; then he would wash his hands and rinse his inkstone. It all looked as if he were going to receive an important guest. Even then he would wait until he had calmed his spirit and composed his thoughts before he would begin to paint.

The idea of capturing the spirit of something, rather than its superficial likeness, has remained an important guiding principle in Chinese painting, and is beautifully expressed by Lo Ta Ching's (fl. c. twelfth century) description of Tsang Wu Yi's untiring efforts to understand the ways of a grasshopper:

Even as a child, I was fond of watching the grasshopper. To begin with, I would put it in a cage and look at it day and night. Then I realized I missed a lot this way. So I started to watch its movements on grass. Then when I started to paint it, I was wont to forget whether I was the grasshopper or the grasshopper was me.

3

The Mustard Seed Garden Manual of Painting

In the previous chapter, we saw how Hsieh Ho's fifth element (a well thought-out composition), and sixth element (learning from the best of tradition), were reconciled in Chinese aesthetic thought with Ching Hao's 'lively vibrancy'. Traditionally, Chinese painters have had a way of doing things that, to those unfamiliar with Chinese culture, may appear more artificial than lively, even verging on the bizarre. One of the painting traditions that may seem peculiar to the uninitiated is the use of stylized devices to represent certain natural objects such as clouds, water, leaves, distant trees, rocks and hills—to name but a few.

These traditions stretch back many centuries, and although the origins of them have not been precisely determined, it seems that traces of stylization can be found on jade carvings dating from as early as the seventh century BC. The earliest known paintings also provide examples of such stylized pictorial representation. In Ku Kai Chih's *Goddess of the Lo River*, dating from about the fourth century AD, the trees clearly show this tendency. Thereafter, it became commonplace to stylize rock texture, river waves, trees, and increasingly complex leaf formations. However, it was not until the Tang Dynasty (AD 618–905) that this art of *ts'un*, meaning stylized textural strokes (mainly on rocks and hills), became a fully integrated part of landscape painting.

The tradition spread to other genres, and many different forms of *ts'un* evolved at the same time as other devices were developed to represent objects in painting. As discussed in the previous chapter, the question of likeness and unlikeness, of verisimilitude and feeling, was central to the Chinese painter's approach to his work. The mastery of a vocabulary of textural devices and representative figures not only became an integral part of the artist's training, it also liberated the artist to capture the spirit of his subject.

However, it was not until the seventeenth century that a comprehensive manual, containing examples of pictorial devices used in painting, was published. The *Chieh Tzu Yuan Hua Chuan* or *Mustard Seed Garden Manual of Painting* appeared in 1679, edited by Wang Kai. It contained a collection of fine woodblock prints, many of which were in colour.

The manual begins with a general theory of the art of painting, with guides to the use of brush and ink and descriptions of different types of paper and colouring materials. The bulk of the book consists of illustrations of 'types' of rocks, trees, mountains, human figures, and so on. It soon became the most widely-used handbook of painting in China, and was acclaimed as a unique summary of the ideals and standards established by masters of the past (Hsieh Ho's sixth element).

Many of the illustrations given in the manual can be described as 'type-forms', in other words, as distillations of the essential reality of each form, achieved through centuries of observation. The observers were men of culture and learning, whose habits of contemplation and visual memory were quickened by their discipline in the writing and reading of Chinese characters. Natural forms were studied not principally for reasons of verisimilitude, but with close reference to their typical and permanent phenomena, to their 'functions' as well as their appearances. Certain general principles were deduced from them, and these in turn were crystallized into the type-forms found in the manual.

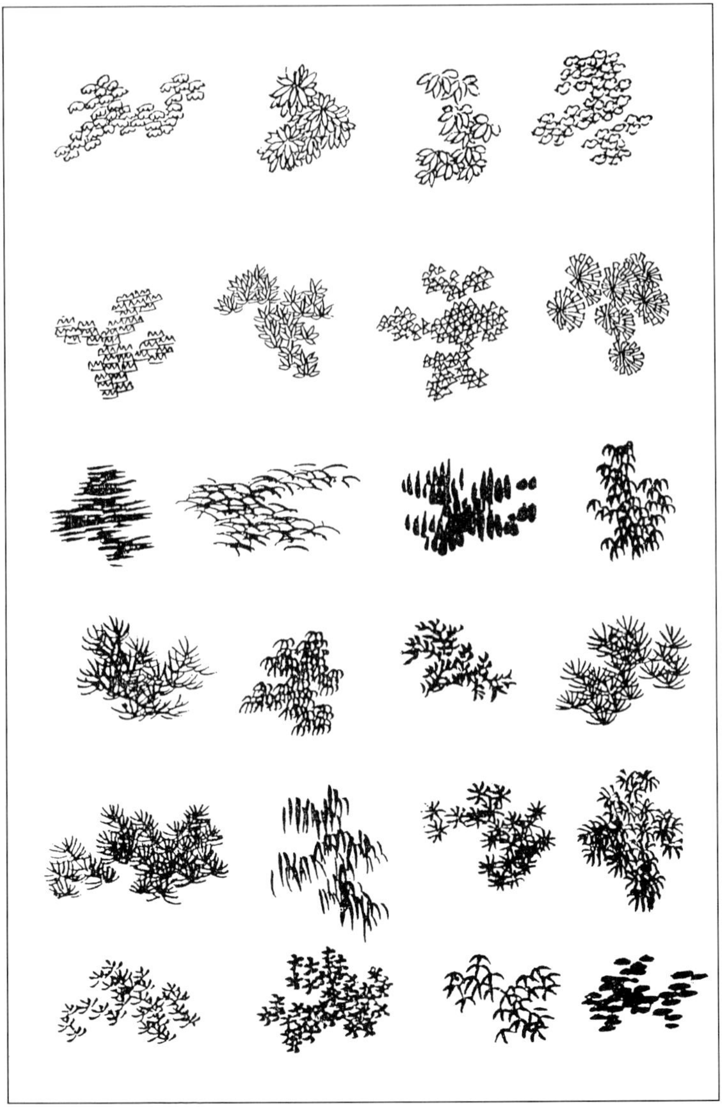

Some type-forms of leaves

Towards the end of the Ming Dynasty (1368–1628), the type-forms had become so firmly established that not only monochrome paintings of bamboo, orchids and such, but also various 'types' of landscape, human figures, birds, fishes and flowers, could be painted directly on silk or paper without preliminary sketches.

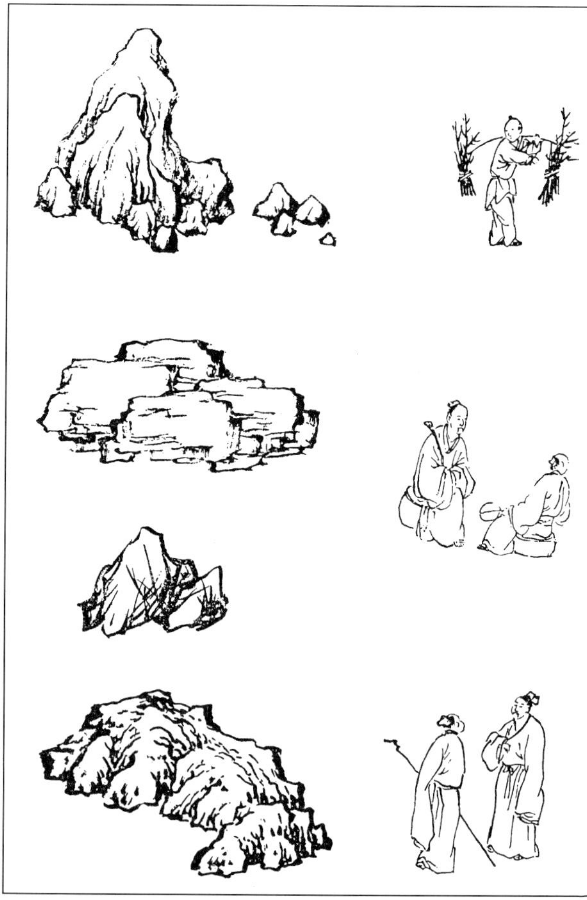

Some type-forms of rocks and figures

For over two centuries, the manual served as a very useful facilitator. Most painters at one time or another turned to it for help, including for example, Chi Pai Shih (1863–1957), who claimed that he owed a great deal to the manual for 'setting him off' on landscape painting. The comment is revealing, since there was a danger that the manual, useful as it was as a reference book for those who worked entirely in traditional idioms, could become stultifying.

The viewer who comes fresh to Chinese painting might also think that the type-forms reduce the landscape genre to a kind of jigsaw puzzle, and that manuals of painting simply encouraged a 'sameness' of production, reflected in the mechanical assembly of manual types. However, composition was not the only element involved. As discussed in Chapter 2, capturing the spirit and 'baring the chest' were equally important requirements for the skilled painter. The way to these lay in adequate spiritual preparation and successful execution of the type-forms. Power and abandon could not be achieved without technical expertise, and this only came from long practise in the art of calligraphy. Anyone who has handled a Chinese brush will realize that virtuosity cannot possibly be achieved without a full command of technique, a long acquaintance with suitable type-forms (both pictorial and literary), and—as a result of these—an openness to inspiration.

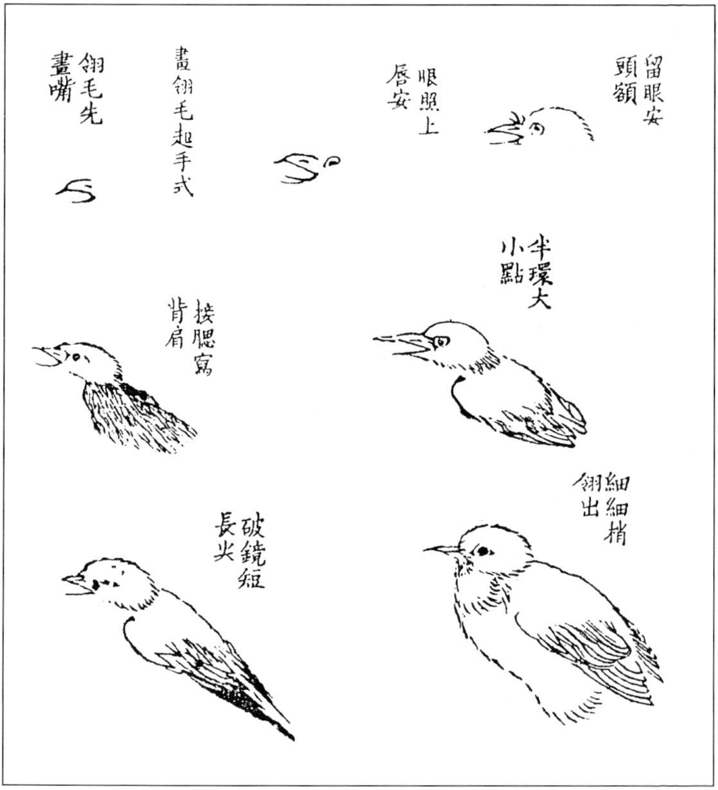

Instructions on how to draw a bird

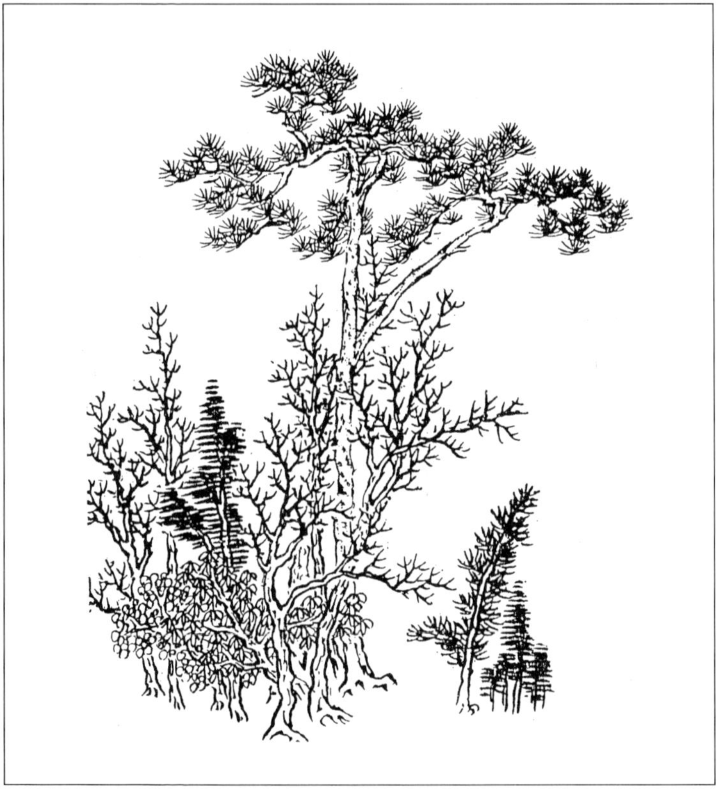

A model grouping of trees

4

Symbolism in Chinese Painting

The Mustard Seed Garden Manual of Painting shows the emphasis placed on well thought-out composition and the use of type-forms in Chinese painting as a way of 'imaging' certain philosophical truths. This traditional use of symbolic types includes a whole range of natural subjects, with the result that many elements of a Chinese painting can be appreciated just as much for their symbolic connotations as for their visual pleasure. In some cases, the painting can be judged good or bad according to its relative success in conveying symbolic values. Their traditional meaning is so strong that it is difficult for the artist to claim symbolism is not his intent. A knowledge of symbolic meanings in Chinese painting will inevitably help the viewer towards a fuller appreciation.

The 'reading' of painting is a natural extension of the calligraphic technique of painting, which was developed during the Song and Yuan Dynasties (tenth to thirteenth centuries) and reached its zenith in the literary circles of the Ming and Qing Dynasties (fourteenth to nineteenth centuries). The monochrome rendering of bamboo, orchids, plum-blossoms, lotuses, and rocks became an art form almost of its own, and was much practised by cultured amateurs and persons of refined taste, particularly since it could be learnt as one learnt to paint or write characters. Monochrome pictures, especially of bamboo, could be done directly on paper or silk without previous sketches. The 'character', as it were, of the subject would be well thought-out and remembered. A painter of bamboos or orchids would not dream of sketching his pictures on the paper first, just as no calligrapher would consider drawing an outline of the characters before writing them. This branch of painting was in a sense scholarly, had a vocabulary, and could be learnt almost by rote. Its technique was mastered in the same way as one learnt to write characters.

Subjects generally considered to have symbolic significance acquired such from famous sayings, from historical events, and above all from inherent qualities observed over many centuries. The following is by no means an exclusive list, but it includes some of the most well-known subjects, along with their symbolic 'truths'.

PLUM-BLOSSOM

The plum-blossom is one of the few flowers that can endure frosty weather. The Chinese scholar therefore regards it as a symbol of fortitude and endurance, making it a very popular subject in Chinese art. A hermit of the eleventh century, Lin Pu, lived on a hill overlooking Hangzhou's famous scenic West Lake. He considered the plum-blossom to be his 'wife'.

BAMBOO

There are many references to the bamboo in the *Book of Songs* compiled by Confucius, but it did not acquire any special significance until the fourth century AD. Scholars admired the bamboo for its 'gentlemanly qualities' of uprightness, humility and unbending loyalty. Seven great scholars of the Eastern Qin Dynasty called themselves 'The Seven Sages of the Bamboo Grove'. In the Tang Dynasty, the great poet Li Po and five other literati called themselves 'Six Recluses among Bamboos near a Rock'.

Wang Hsien Chih, son of the great calligrapher Wang Hsi Chih, once remarked that he could not live without bamboo for even a single day.

CHRYSANTHEMUM

From early times, the chrysanthemum was seen as a life-prolonging herb and effective against rheumatism. In the fourth century AD, it became closely associated with the recluse T'ao Ch'ien. The 'Four Gentlemen' of Chinese art are the chrysanthemum, the plum-blossom, the orchid, and the bamboo.

THE FIVE PURE THINGS

These are the bamboo, the plum-blossom, the pine, the moon, and water.

THE CRANE

The crane is a symbol of longevity. It is especially associated with the philosopher Lao Tze (fifth century BC), who is often depicted riding on its back. The Song Dynasty poet, Lin Pu, called his sons 'cranes' and his wife 'plum-blossom'.

THE THREE FRIENDS OF WINTER

These are the pine, bamboo and plum-blossom, and they are considered as friends of winter since they continue to grow in the cold season.

THE PEACH

The peach symbolizes immortality, since the myth holds that the God of Longevity was born from a peach.

THE LOTUS

The lotus is a symbol of purity, its leaves emerging undefiled from the muddy pond. It is one of the central symbols in both Buddhist and Taoist belief, and its purity reaches beyond natural things to a divine order or 'truth', signified by its being chosen to support the world or to lie at the heart of the celebrated Buddhist moonstone.

MANDARIN DUCKS

Mandarin ducks are a symbol of harmony and marital bliss, since they are often seen in pairs.

THE CARP

According to Chinese mythology, once the carp gets past the rapids of the Dragon Gate it changes into a dragon. It was therefore used to signify success in the Imperial Examination, once so vital to the careers of the literati class.

THE GOURD

The gourd is a symbol of mystery and is the emblem of one of the Eight Immortals, Iron Crutch Li. The Chinese saying 'What is in your gourd?' means 'What are you hiding?'

THE WILD DUCK

The wild duck or *yen* is a migratory bird; it has therefore come to symbolize the carrier of messages from distant lands. The phrase 'to communicate by wild duck' means to exchange letters.

THE BROOM

The broom sweeps away all cares and worries. It is a symbol of insight and wisdom, being especially associated with the poet-monk of the Tang Dynasty, Shih-te.

Only a small part of the painting is shown here. The other parts of the scroll include five court ladies with their pets, a crane and two small dogs, possibly Pekinese.

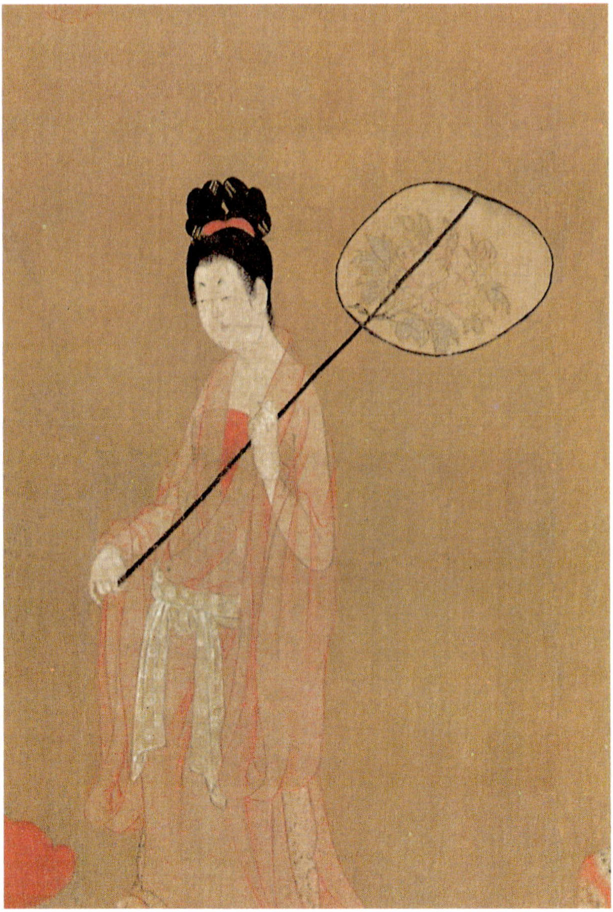

Court Ladies
By Chou Fang (Tang Dynasty)
Part of a hand scroll

The painting depicts a hen and her chicks picking up food in the field. Fine brushwork with rich but not gaudy colours.

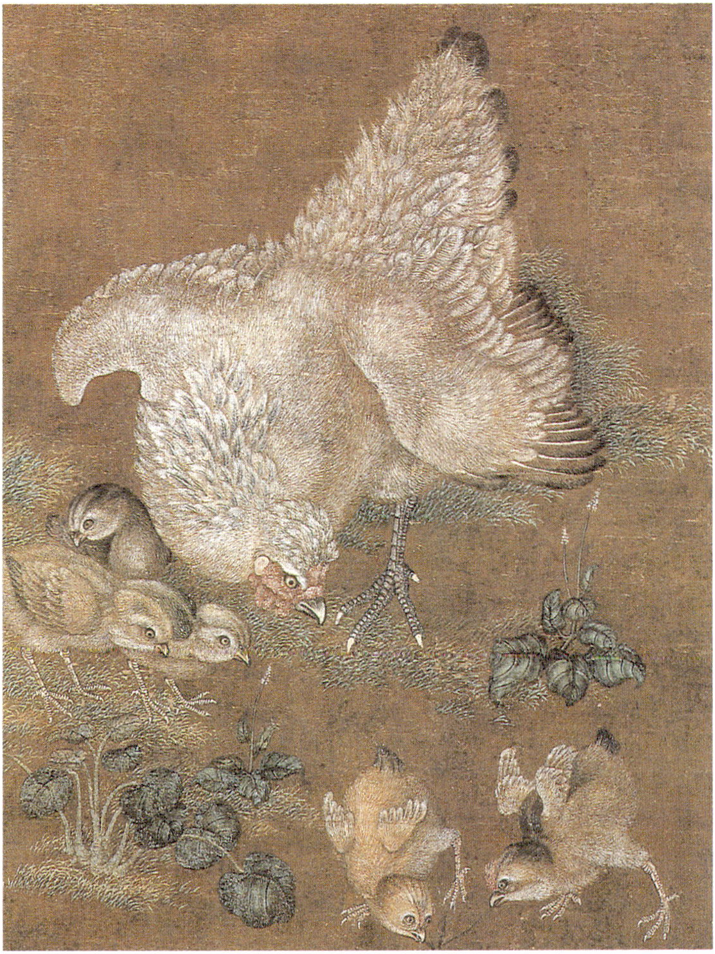

Hen and Chicks
By Chu Bai (Song Dynasty)
Hanging scroll

Strong mineral colours were commonly used during the time when this was painted.

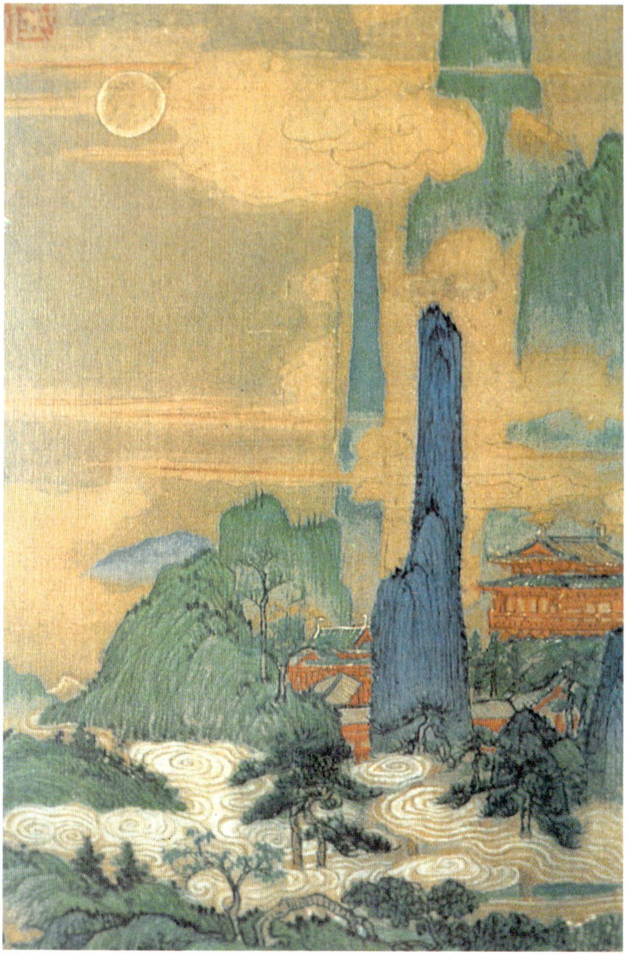

Habitat of the Immortals
Attributed to Chao Po Chu (Southern Song Dynasty)
Fan-shaped silk leaf

Notice the many treasures of a scholar's studio laid out on the large table. It was unusual for females to take part in a male-dominated event, but daughters of the wealthy, highly-placed or learned were sometimes allowed. In the picture, three scholars are watching the lady while others are looking at a scroll.

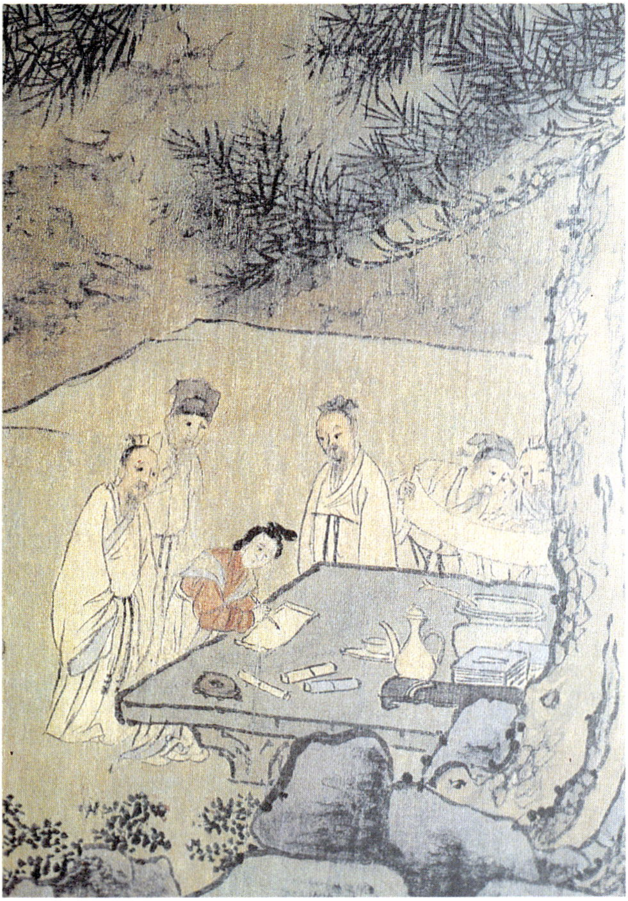

Artists Gathering
By Tai Chin (1388–1462)

The painter was an all-round artist. He was the most senior of the 'Four Masters of Ming', the others being Wen Cheng Ming, Tang Yin and Chiu Ying.

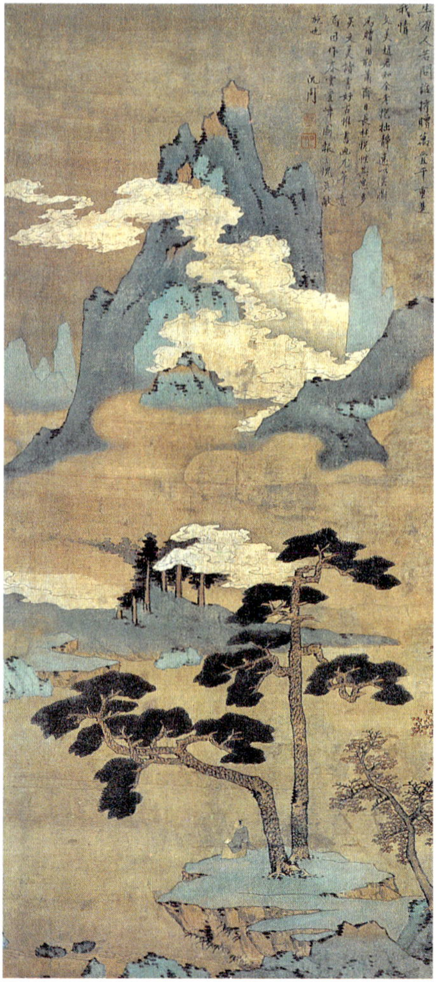

Scholar Reading
By Shen Chou (1427–1509)
Hanging scroll

Sun was a flower-bird-insect specialist. This picture of a cicada clinging to a small branch was done on silk, using the 'boneless' technique. Put simply, 'boneless' means applying ink and colour directly on the painting surface without first making structural outlines.

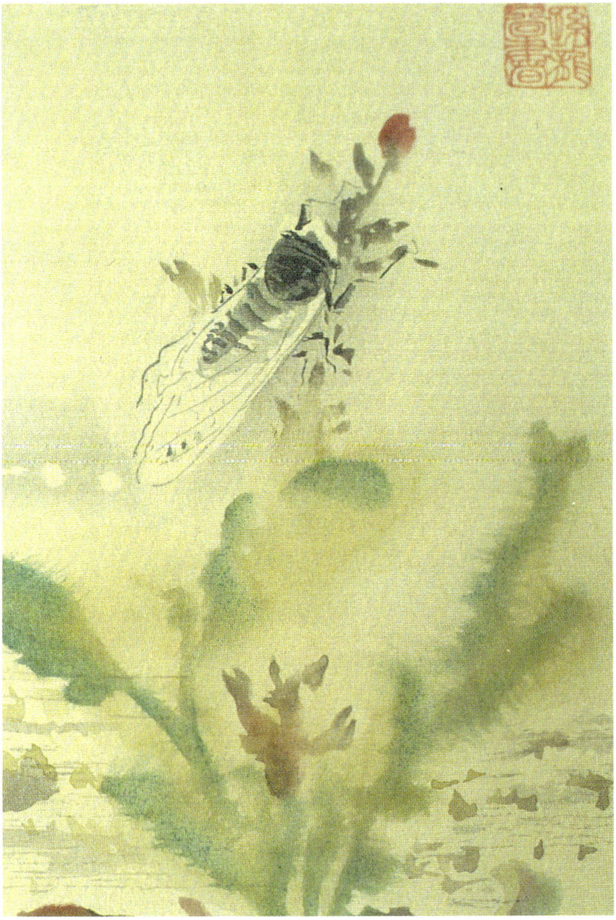

Cicada
By Sun Lung (sixteenth century)

The picture may well be an illustration of one of Li Po's poems that reads:

You ask why I choose to live amongst these hills.
I smile without offering an answer—my heart at ease.
Flowing waters and fallen flowers go without a trace.
A different sky and earth here—not of this world.

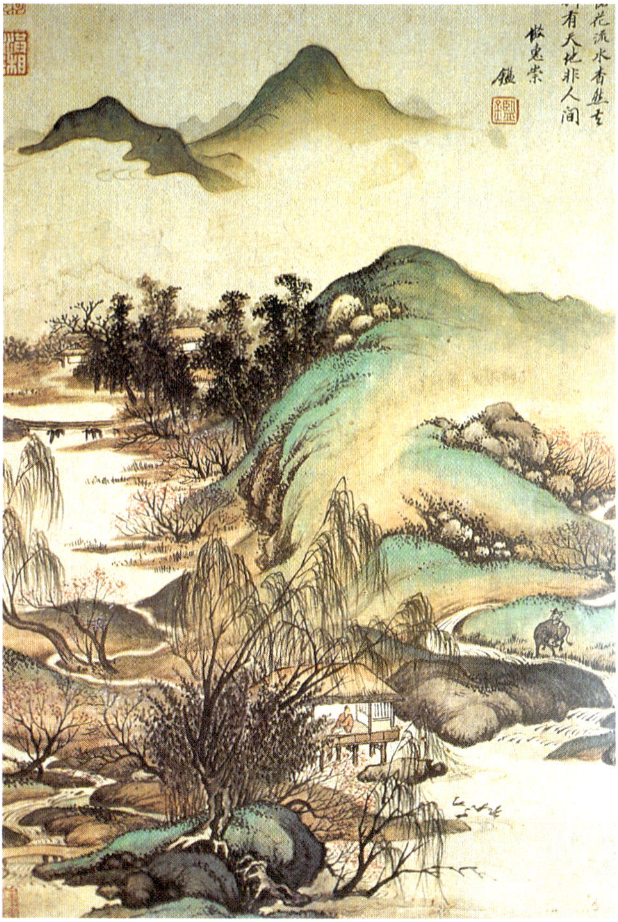

Landscape
By Wang Chien (1589–1677), one of the 'Four Wangs' of the Qing Dynasty.
Album leaf

An excellent example of a 'collaborative painting'. As the terms implies, it is a painting done by many hands: in this case, by Wang Hui together with thirty of his friends, each identifiable by signature and seal placed directly over the parts they painted. Collaborative paintings are still popular, usually being done during literary or artistic gatherings, and occasionally they are undertaken impromptu, each artist adding to what is there with astounding results.

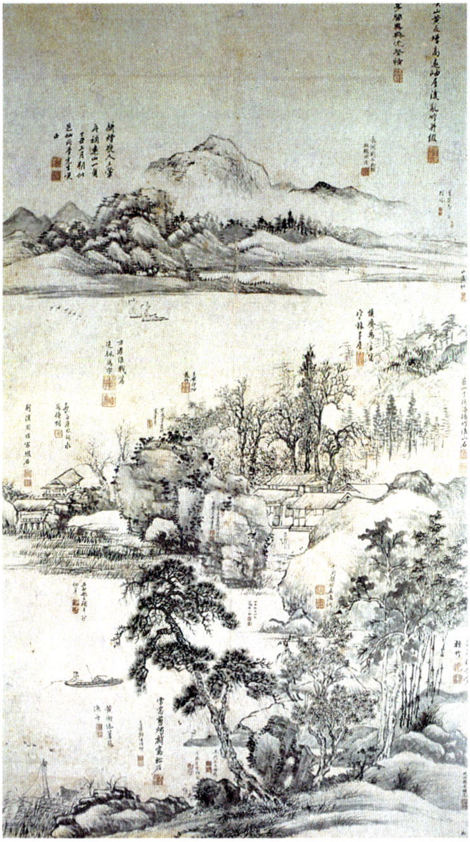

Landscape
By various artists (1697)
Hanging scroll

Here one of the ducks is diving in play or in search of food, while the younger duck watches. The picture may be an illustration of a line in one of the poems by Su Shih, the Song Dynasty poet: 'Ducks are the first to feel the warmth of the river in spring.' The extraordinary deftness of Hua's brush is best shown in this picture, which may be usefully compared with Ding Yan Yung's painting of the same theme.

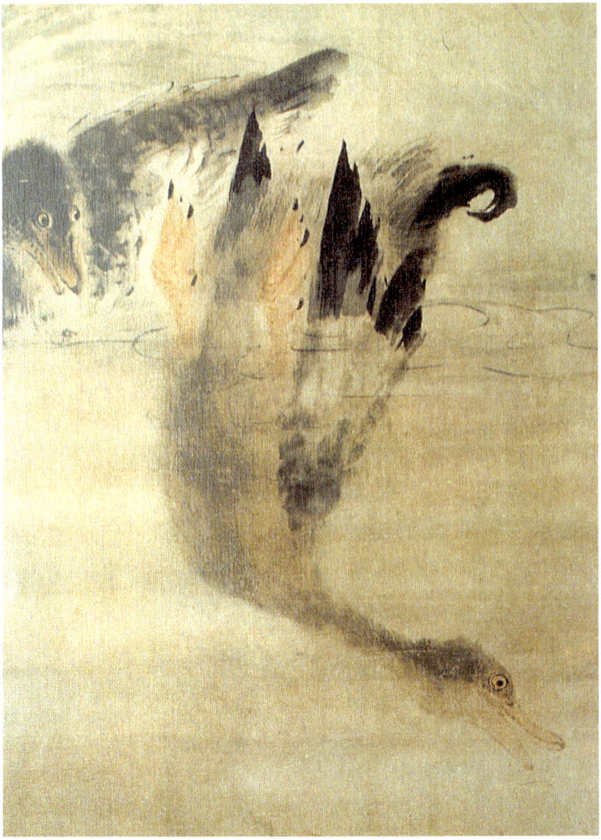

Two Ducks
By Hua Yen (1682–1786), one of the 'Eight Eccentrics of Hangzhou'

The painter is best known for his 'splash-ink' wild ducks, a speciality of his that has never been excelled. The reeds are 'written' in the way bamboo leaves are, spare but full of inner force.

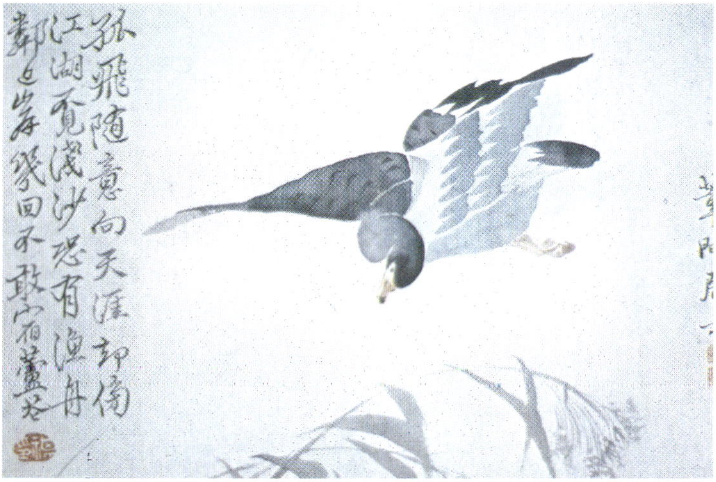

Wild Duck in Flight
By Bian Shou Min (1684–1752)
Album leaf

Painted by one of the 'Eight Eccentrics of Yangzhou', this album leaf is a fine example of the fusion of calligraphy with painting. Notice how the group of characters drives a wedge between the two bamboo shoots. The drift of the inscription is that a real painter finds sustenance from things ordinary people avoid.

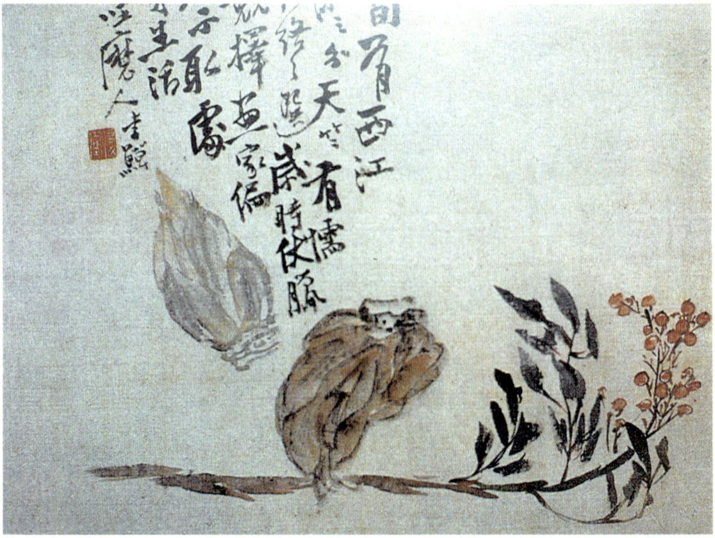

Winter Bamboo Shoots
By Li Chan (1696–1762)
Album leaf

The painter is best known as Giuseppe Castiglione, an Italian missionary who came to China in 1715. He soon became court painter, a position he served under three emperors: Kang Hsi, Yung Cheng, and Chien Lung. This picture of horses shows how he attempts to combine Western realism with Chinese convention and technique.

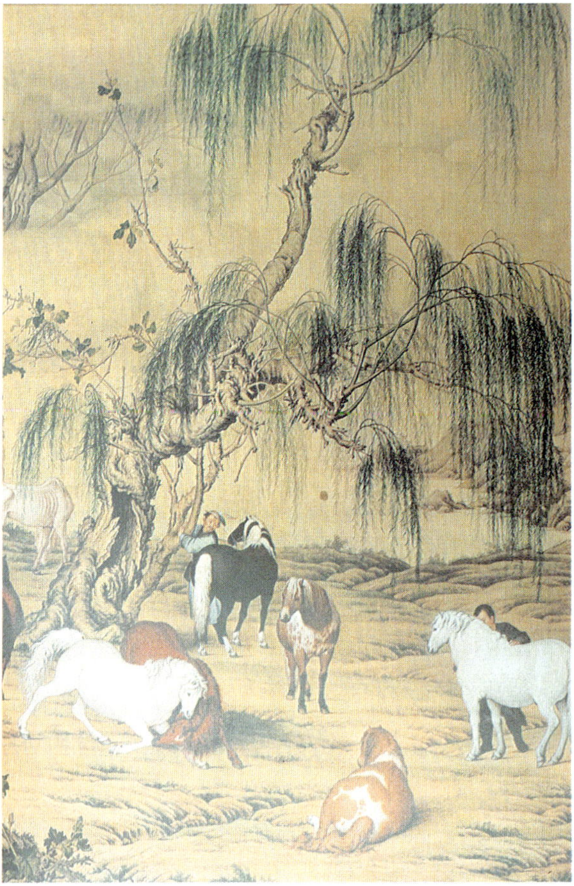

Horses
By Lang Shi Ning (1688–1766)
Hanging scroll

A charming arrangement by a specialist in flowers and insects. Chu, of Kwangtung Province, was a pioneer and leader of the Lingnam school of painting. He was particularly well known for his skill in the application of white pigment (mainly powder) on a wet surface for special effects.

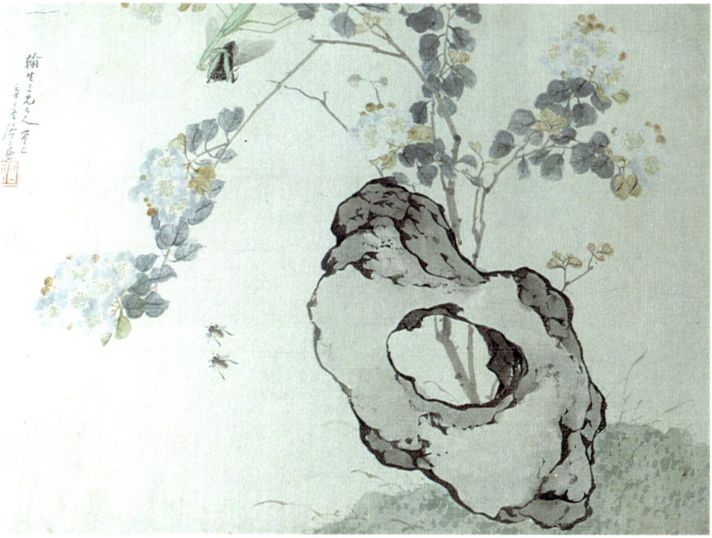

Rock, Flowers and Bees
By Chu Lian (1828–1904)
Fan

A typical literati painting with clearly articulated brushwork, evincing great spontaneity and freshness. Note the large dots in varying shades of ink, representing leaves, and the calligraphic lines shaping the kiosk—both indicate that the painting was 'written' on a swift, creative impulse.

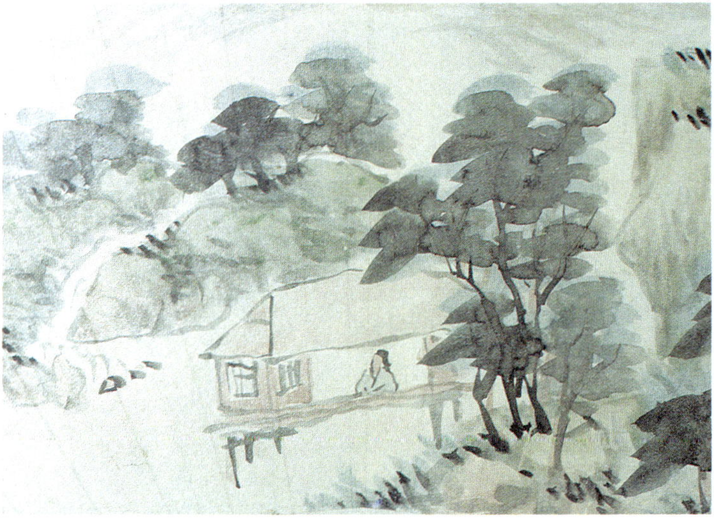

Landscape with Scholar in a Water-kiosk
By Wu Yung-yun (fl. late nineteenth century)

This striking composition is typical of the painter's style: simple and 'abbreviated'. The brushwork is well controlled. The picture is characterised by a child-like naiveté.

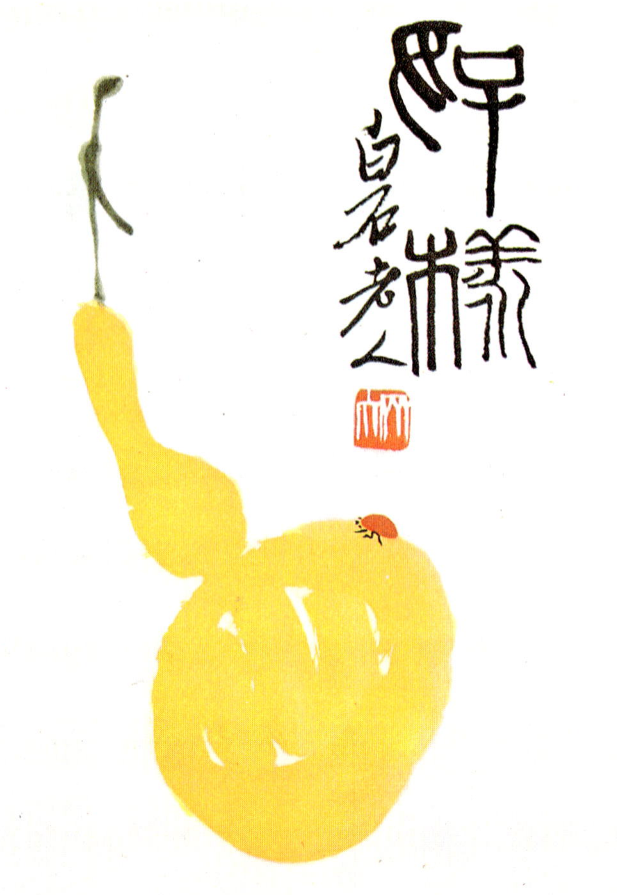

Bottle Gourd and Ladybird
By Chi Pai Shih (1862–1957)
Album leaf

An unusual composition by someone who was famous for his command of the brush. It was done when the eighty nine year-old artist was on the verge of blindness. Although Huang could not see what he was painting, it is believed that his hand was guided by the calligraphic brush technique he had developed and mastered over eighty years of practice.

The inscription is characteristic, being an observation on painting techniques and development. In summary it reads:

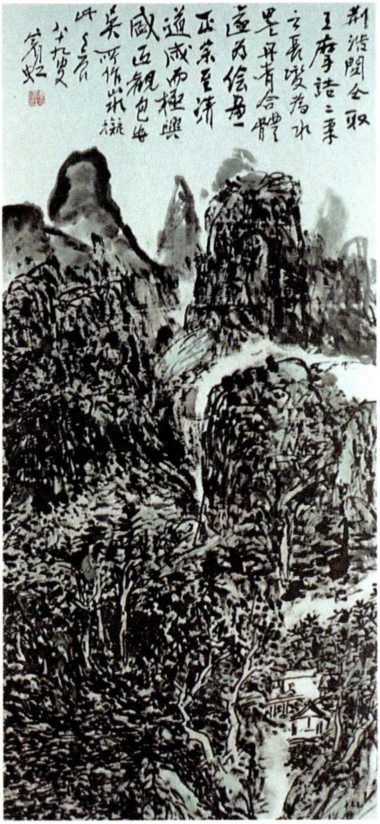

Ching Hao and Kwan Tung absorbed the strong points in the art of Wang Wei and the two Lis. By a fusion of ink, water and colour they created a mainstream in the art of painting. The reigns of Tao Kwang and Hsien Feng in the Qing Dynasty saw the movement in its fullest blossoming. I try my hand here after seeing the landscapes by Pao An Wu. Bin–hong at eighty nine.

Landscape
By Huang Bin–hong (1864–1955)
Hanging scroll

5

Inscriptions in Chinese Painting

As mentioned in Chapter 1, the inclusion of inscriptions and seals was a natural extension of the calligraphic basis of Chinese painting. Since painters were also scholars, it was almost inevitable that painting should not only come to include type-forms and overt symbols, but also written prose and poetry. Sometimes the inscription is very little—the date of the painting and the person to whom it is given or dedicated—but it could also include a poem, a description of the subject, an exposition of the theory and technique of painting in general, or of the tones and shades (the play of opposites in the composition of a type-form, for example) in that particular work of art. Any proper appreciation of Chinese painting requires some understanding of this essential component.

This is particularly true of the paintings of the Tang Dynasty and onwards. In the early days of Chinese art, signatures and seals were seldom, if ever, used. They can first be observed on paintings scholars attribute to the Tang Dynasty, and were very small characters hidden between rocks or other objects. Sometimes, if the painter considered his calligraphic technique less than presentable, they were even written on the back of the paper. The inscribing of dates came into fashion in the Song Dynasty, when Su Shih (AD 1037–1101) began to write a few lines on the front of his work.

Both tradition and training dictated that Chinese painters were also literary people (in many cases scholar-literati in government service), and so the temptation to add something, especially in the form of a poem written in one's perfected calligraphic hand, was often irresistible. The practice became ingrained over the course of many centuries, with the result that artists who were proficient in all the three aspects of painting, poetry and calligraphy, were described as possessing the 'three perfections'. In the Song Dynasty, poetic inscriptions on painting reached the status of a literary (and not solely pictorial) genre, when Su Shih and his friend Huang T'ing Chien (AD 1050–1100) advanced the theory that poetic inspiration derives from the same source as pictorial inspiration. Poetry and painting came to be spoken of as equals, on the same level of artistic endeavour.

By the twelfth century, anthologies of poetic inscriptions were being published. During the Ming Dynasty such inscriptions became the norm, and by the time of the Qing Dynasty inscriptions not only occupied large parts of paintings, they were also so placed and written as to be aesthetically bound up with the visual experience of the work. They shed light on the artist's purpose or basic idea, helping the viewer to see the artist's intentions as clearly as possible.

They also included critical remarks, being written just as often by fellow artists, collectors and friends, as by the painters themselves. They often had a discursive element, providing a kind of commentary on the work or an eulogy on the painter. The Emperor Chien Lung of the Qing Dynasty was well-known for his habit of making inscriptions on many of the paintings in the imperial collection (unfortunately the published ones are not very revealing). This habit has helped scholars to trace the authenticity of a particular work of art; although it may be possible to fake a person's painting style, it is much more difficult to imitate his calligraphy.

Seals too became an integral part of the painting's concept, a fashion that began tentatively in the Yuan Dynasty

(1206–1341) when Wang Mien, best known for his paintings of plum-blossoms, first used stone for seal-carving. This was revolutionary—before then artists and scholars had been dependent on professional seal-carvers, who used harder materials like jade and bronze. It was not long before literary people, including painters, began to take up seal-carving as an art in itself, and indeed it became equated in the aesthetic scale of things with poetry. Anyone who excelled in writing, painting and seal-carving could also proudly claim to be a possessor of the 'three perfections'.

The following are examples of paintings in which seals and inscriptions play a prominent part. The inscriptions are translated.

The inscription on the painting below is aesthetically bound up with the visual experience of the work. The superb calligraphy is strategially placed on two rock surfaces and the viewer enjoys the inscription as much as the other parts.

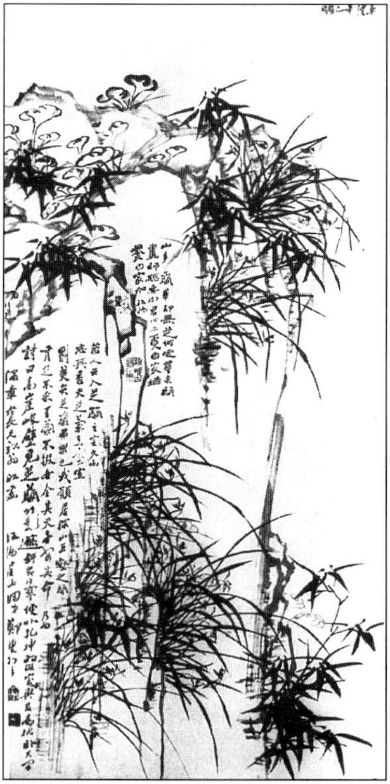

There are orchids on the hills, but no irises.
'Where can you find them?' I ask of the painter.
'You'll find them within yourself—
You have cultivated them, and you know that.'
The ancients say, 'After being in a room of orchids for some time,
You'll cease to notice their fragrance.'
Indeed, to have orchids and irises in the room will enhance its beauty;
But to the orchids and irises, it means nothing.
I would wish to live deep in the mountains, but I will not pick orchids and irises.
Between us, we will preserve what Heaven has ordained, and feel contented with what we are.
I have written a poem to celebrate that:
'I look up, and some orchids and irises can be seen
Bright against the bamboo's shade on a winter day.
0, let the universe be our bedchamber
And we can all live happily in its immensity.'

Orchids and Irises
by Cheng Hsieh (1693–1765)
Hanging scroll

A scroll in which the painting and the inscription play an equally important role, not only in the size of the areas they cover, but also in their impact on the viewer. Note also the number of seals. The inscription reads:

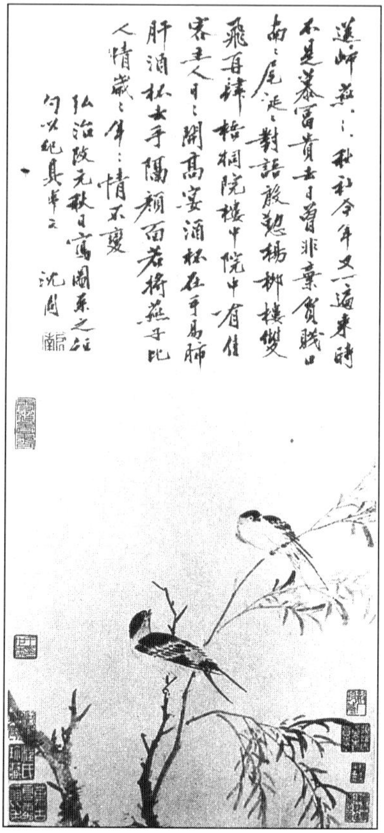

Farewell swallows!
Swallows, farewell!
It is autumn again
And time to repeat
Your yearly migration.
Coming not for wealth or rank,
You leave not to escape poverty.
Twittering, wagging your tails
Intimately, you chat in the willow-chambers,
And fly in pairs and linger in the Wutung Court,
Where mine host daily his favourite friends entertains.
With cup in hand, they pledge eternal friendship;
When separated they soon forget each other.
Oh, how much more constant the swallows are
Who unfailingly return year after year.

Two Swallows
By Shen Chou (1427–1509)
Hanging scroll

A typical 'literati' painting, in which both the brushwork and the calligraphy are superb. A scion of the Qing imperial family, Pu chose a career as a painter. The peace of mind he achieved, although not completely free of disenchantment, is well expressed in the form of the poem he wrote to accompany the scholar:

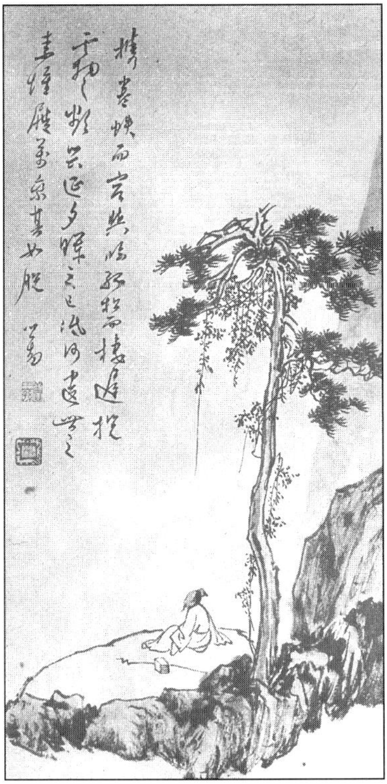

I take my books and sit here without a care,
Dallying with a lonesome pine under its shade.
Perceiving how rapidly the clouds and everything change,
I invite the evening sun to stay a little longer.
My pure hermit heart—What does it say?
Ten thousand chariots are but old shoes to me.

Landscape with Sitting Scholar
By Pu Hsin Yu (1896–1963)
Hanging scroll

In Chinese aesthetics, ink has five 'hues' or colour tones. When skilfully used, these can give great pleasure to the discerning viewer. Shih Tao was well known for his unconventional views on painting techniques, as is suggested by this rather cryptic inscription about a poor monk who could not afford proper materials:

Huai Su studied calligraphy and planted banana trees so that their leaves could be used as a substitute for paper. The ink runs profusely when it rains. I believe this painting of mine images that situation.

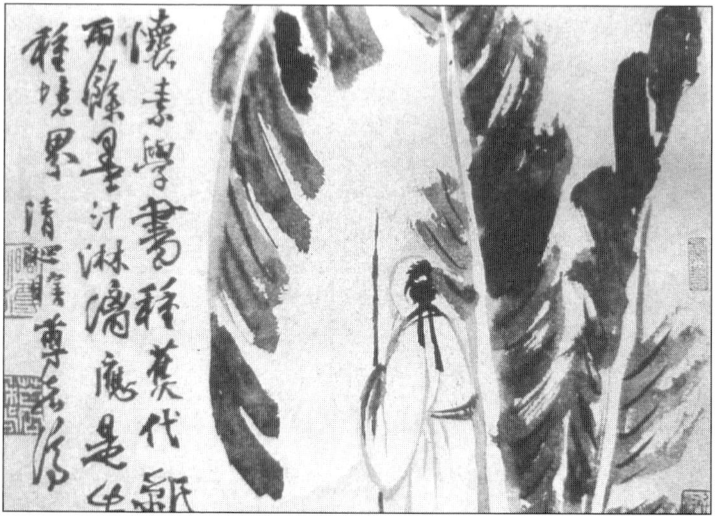

Banana Tree
By Shih Tao (1641–1717), one of the 'Four Monks of Early Qing'
Album leaf

6

Chinese Landscape Painting

CHINESE painting is particularly associated with landscapes, perhaps even more so than in the art of other Asian countries, an emphasis that has its roots in the various religious and philosophical sources of Chinese culture. The idea that wisdom and peace can be found in the viewing of mountains and rivers, indeed the vitality of various forms of nature and their connection with the spirit world, is central to both Taoism and Buddhism.

However, traditional Chinese landscape painting can appear monotonous to the uninitiated. The viewer can easily be put off by the fact that nature is not rendered as the eye or the camera might see it. As discussed in the previous chapters, verisimilitude is not the Chinese painter's priority, and so in order to enjoy a landscape painting the viewer must be ready to accept, or at least understand certain conventions and stylizations. For example, the landscape artist represents a scene as if it is being viewed from a height or a distance, or even from far below. In other words, he does not employ a stationary or single viewpoint; the picture may include things he sees as he goes on his way, or those that would not otherwise be seen at the same moment in time or space. According to the angle of his vision, the landscapes he paints fall into three types: from a bird's-eye view, he creates a 'deep-distance' composition; from an eye-level view, he creates a 'flat-distance' composition; and from below, he creates a 'high-distance' composition. Without an understanding of these modes, Chinese landscape painting will certainly disappoint the viewer.

Type-forms too can be an impediment to appreciation, since their use may seem merely mechanical and repetitious. However, such criticism ignores the finesse and individuality involved in both choice, composition and execution. For example, the texturing of rocks and mountains requires 'shading' or 'moulding' strokes from the brush. This process is termed *ts'un* (see Chapter 3) or 'wrinkles', a term originating from cracks caused by the skin's exposure to extreme cold. Over a long period of time, a variety of *ts'un* strokes was developed, each requiring the brush to adopt different angles and techniques to produce different effects.

Proficiency in the art of *ts'un* became indispensable to landscape painters. In his *Treatise on Landscape Painting*, Shih Tao (1630–1707) wrote:

> *Ts'un* serves the purpose of showing the 'facial' features and texture. Since mountains have numerous forms, their facial features are also different...Therefore there are different kinds of *ts'un*, such as curling-cloud *ts'un*, axe-chop *ts'un*, loose-rope *ts'un*, demon-face *ts'un*, skull-like *ts'un* ...These are different *ts'un* strokes. They must vary as the shapes and features of the peaks demand.

A contemporary of Shih Tao's, Ta Chung-kuang (fl.1652), wrote a long poem on painting in which he devoted a whole section to a discussion of *ts'un* strokes in the depiction of mountains and peaks:

> While hills and rocks depend on *ts'un* strokes to give them form and texture, over-eagerness to use them produces artificiality; outlines denote the contour of mountains and peaks, and *ts'un* strokes represent the texture of earth and rocks...When *ts'un* strokes are not sufficient, the deficiency can be remedied by a heavy wash; when *ts'un* strokes are adequate, a light wash will add interest to the picture; the loose-rope *ts'un* is vibrant, the hemp-fibre *ts'un* is quiet,

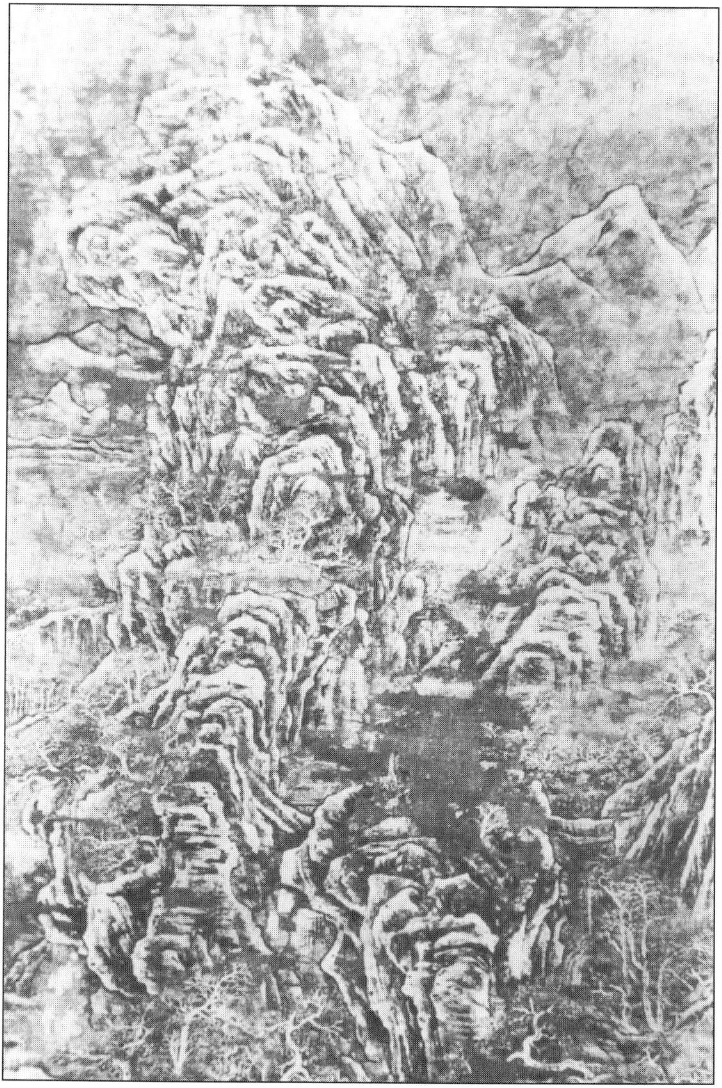

Landscape
By Ching Hao (ninth to tenth century)

the ragged-grass *ts'un* gives a feeling of simplicity, while the ox-hair *ts'un* gives an air of refinement... *Ts'un* strokes may be likened to windswept rushes or grass heavy with dew, clear as rain seeping through crevices on the wall, or subtle as objects viewed through a silken gauze...When different colours vie for superiority, the spirit of a landscape is spoiled; aiming to be different, brush and ink can create grotesque results. It is easy to produce fantastic forms, but they soon exhaust the sense of novelty. It is most difficult to create beauty out of ordinary objects, but when that is achieved, one never tires of the results.

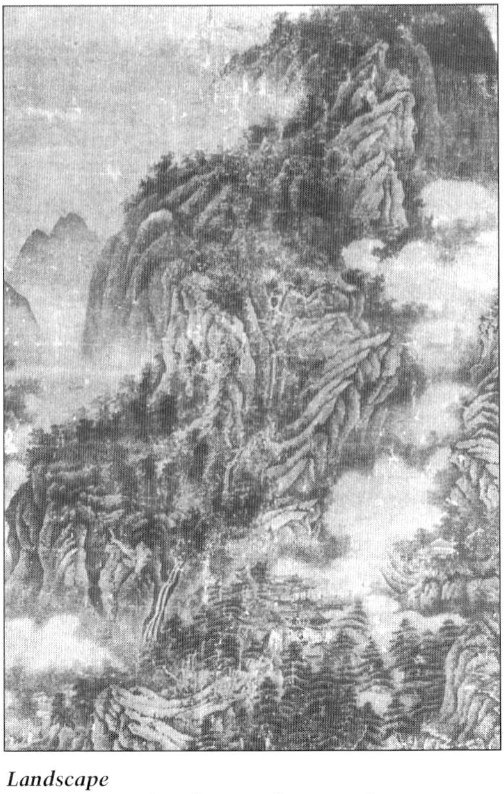

Landscape
By Kuan Tung (ninth to tenth century)

This is a long way from the individualist expressionism of Western painting, but there is nevertheless both variety and intense observation involved in the *ts'un* tradition. Artists of different geographical regions have produced their own versions of *ts'un* as convenient formulae for depicting local landscape objects. Indeed, the development of different versions of the technique was the subject of a painstaking study made by the Japanese geologist, Takashima Hokkai (1850–1931), published as *Essentials of Mountain Painting*, with a Chinese translation by Fu Pao-shih. The following is an extract from the book:

> The ability to execute the contour and *ts'un* is the primary prerequisite for success in the painting of mountains and peaks. *Ts'un* originates from observation of nature: the contour depicts light and shade as elevation and depth of hills and rocks; *ts'un* strokes represent their density, cracks, fissures, strata, and so on. They are the unique invention of Chinese artists through the ages.

One of the greatest landscape painters of all time, Huang Bin-hong (1864–1955), declared that the ancients usually used short strokes to form rocks and hills, sometimes so short that they were like dots. In the management of *ts'un*, he added, the important thing is orderliness, so that when the strokes meet 'they do not kick against, but make way for each other'. He also likened the *ts'un* strokes to those of calligraphy, or to pole-coolies on the road who go out of their way not to collide with each other. This view was echoed by the late Chang Da-Chien (1889–1983) in his *Painting Models*:

> There are no hard and fast rules governing *ts'un*, and the artist is not obliged to adopt any particular type as long as he finds it suitable for the circumstance. For example, Tung Yuan used the hemp-fibre *ts'un* because of its resemblance to the mountains south of the

Yangtze River, which generally have more topsoil than bare rock. Also, they are usually covered with a luxuriant growth of trees and bushes. On the other hand, Fan Kuan's landscapes are full of examples of *ts'un*, such as 'pulling-nail-out-of-the-mud', 'rain-splashing-at-the-wall', and 'demon-face', because he was depicting mountains of North China such as Tai Hang and Hwang Wu, which are rocky and devoid of weeds and mosses. If the two masters were to exchange their respective *ts'un* methods, one wonders what their landscapes would have looked like. Therefore, in my opinion, one should use any particular *ts'un* at one's own discretion, rather than tie oneself to any pedantic rule.

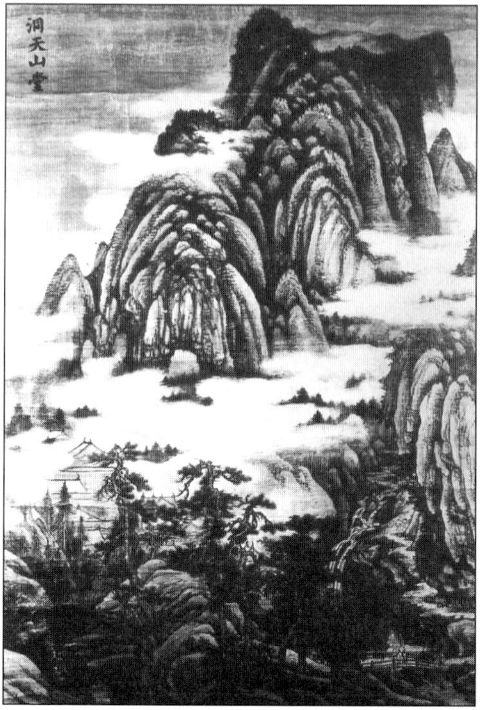

Landscape
By Tung Yuan (907–960)

A discussion of *ts'un* and examples of type-forms of rocks and leaves were included in Chapter 3. Trees were a much more difficult type-form to create. An idea of the general principles of tree painting can best be gained from the teaching models of Lu Yan Shao, a contemporary Chinese painter. Some of the models drawn by Lu himself are reproduced here, along with a summary of his explanatory notes.

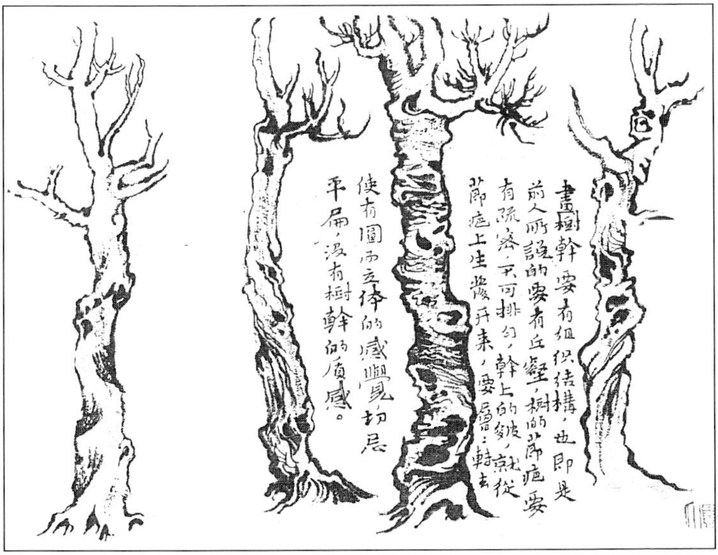

Tree trunks

Every tree trunk has its own organisation and structure, which the ancients called 'mounds and gullies'. Knars on the trunks should be unevenly distributed. The wrinkle-lines should spread out from these knars in such a way as to give a sense of solidity to the trunk, avoiding 'flatness'.

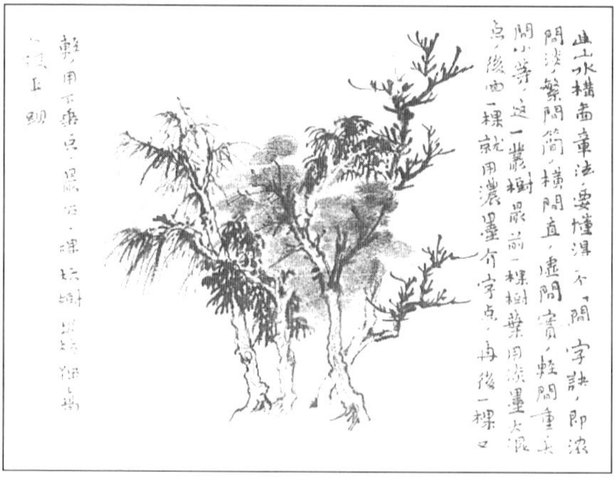

Contrast and leaves

In landscape composition the key-word to excellence is 'contrast': the intense in contrast with the diffuse, the complex in contrast with the simple, the horizontal in contrast with the vertical, emptiness in contrast with substance, light in contrast with heavy, big in contrast with small...Thus behind the pale patches are the dark leaves, behind which are again pale long hanging leaves.

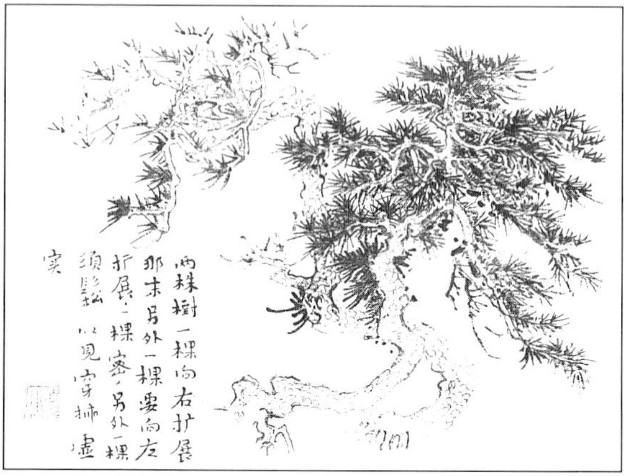

Balance and trees

If one pair of the trees leans towards the right, then the other should lean towards the left. If one tree is densely leaved, then the other should be sparsely leaved, so as to achieve a balance of weight and intensity and liveliness.

7
Brush-ink

BRUSH-INK, or *bi-mo*, is without doubt the most fundamental element of all those mentioned by Hsieh Ho and Ching Hao as forming the basis of Chinese painting, and it is the one that has most differentiated Chinese art from Western traditions. Even nowadays, it is the focus of ongoing controversy between 'traditionalist' and 'modernist' Chinese painters. Traditionally, *bi-mo* means expressive brushwork combined with good ink tonality, but this apparently simple formula has left ample room for debate.

Since Chinese painting has such a close relationship with calligraphy, there are those who argue that a painting cannot be fully appreciated without a knowledge of the Chinese language and, therefore, of the art of calligraphy itself. Only by knowing how to apply the brush oneself, say the purists, can one be sensitive to brushwork and ink tonality. Other painters and scholars are less rigorous. Ideally, they say, one should have a feel for the brush to understand the complexity and finesse of the painter-calligrapher's skill, but it is quite possible to enjoy the texture of a painting for its own sake, regardless of the relationship of a brush stroke with its precise calligraphic counterpart. Indeed, they claim that brushwork has an independent function of its own.

Since most great painters of the past were also very good calligraphers, it is logical to think that proficiency in calligraphy is very helpful in learning to paint, but it is not impossible that someone who knows little Chinese can produce quality brushwork by contemplating as many traditional masterpieces as possible, and using them as models in the practise of his or her art. In other words, although *bi-mo* may be an intricate skill to master, it does have a language of its own—one that can be painstakingly learnt. As Tung Chi-chang (1555–1636) said:

> Few people understand *bi-mo*. But can a painting really be totally devoid of these two things? Simply put, a painting that has only outline but no textural strokes (*ts'un*) is one that has no *bi*; one that has textural strokes but nothing to indicate light and shade, weight and direction, is one that has no *mo*. A brush stroke may be a line, a dot, a curve, a hook, or a blot of any shape, characterised by a rhythmic alternation of thickness and thinness with each stroke, or a multiplicity of them, providing light and shade and contributing charm to the painting. In addition to their function of depicting objects, brush strokes possess an independent value of their own as a means of expression.

The brush stroke may be made with light or heavy ink, a wet or dry brush, an even or varying pressure, a brush held perpendicularly or at an angle. It is the basic structural element of a painting. Swift or slow, delicate or heavy, brush strokes are valued for their own sake, often bearing an imprint as personal as the artist's own handwriting. They are the means by which type-forms are both rendered and transcended. The Chinese painter uses them in an immense variety of ways. He can suggest plasticity by thickening or thinning the brush contours; the same contours can be used to convey the undulating movements of, for example, drapery, without any recourse to the descriptive light used by Western artists (this is especially true of landscape painting). It is difficult, however, to define exactly how all these effects are achieved, and what distinguishes good brushwork and ink tonality from the merely mediocre.

One of the best guides to the subject is Huang Bin-hong (1864–1955), a painter who had first-hand experience of many important Chinese works of art, since from 1935 to 1937 he was an authenticator of paintings in the Palace Museum in Beijing. In his book *Huang Bin-hong's Thoughts on Painting*—a synthesis of the theories of the past—he wrote:

One principal quality of good brushwork is *ping*. To achieve *ping*, one should write as if drawing with an awl on a pool of sand, while one's mind is placid and unruffled. The result is smoothness without dullness or stiffness. A line made with a brush should have 'waves', and each wave should itself be punctuated by minor waves. This is the way to avoid monotony. The brush should produce a 'roundness' like that made by bending a lady's hairpin. Ugly corners should be avoided. Brush strokes should be deliberate, not casual. They should be weighty like the weight of a stone falling from a height, not like fallen leaves driven by the wind.

One is again reminded here of Kuo Ju-Hsu's father 'calming his spirit' before painting. There is a philosophical readiness, an openness to inspiration about these waves of Huang Bin-hong. However, dexterity, strength and elegance of strokes *(bi)* should ideally be accompanied by a corresponding virtuosity in the control of ink. Huang went on to distinguish *mo*, or the various uses of ink, as follows:

Heavy ink, which depends on the quality of the ink itself; light ink, which according to the number of applications, gives different shades and gradations; broken ink, which involves the use of heavy ink on light ink while the latter is still moist, or light ink on heavy ink while the latter is still moist; splash ink, which is a process of painting a picture based on the image made by ink splashed on the painting surface; dry ink, an effect produced by drawing a dry brush over and between patches of heavy and light ink; overnight ink, which can be successfully used only by one whose expertise is such that the residual ink sediments can be made to look good.

This was not a theoretical list: in addition to careful brushwork, Huang Bin-hong believed that a painting could not be considered good unless it included at least three of the ink methods described above.

The following examples show how the expert use of *bi-mo* contributes to the success of a painting.

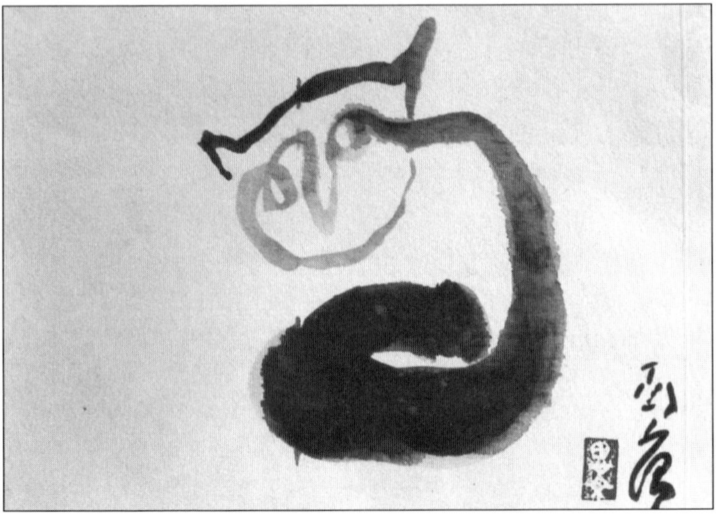

Cat
By Ding Yan Yung (1905–1978)
Album leaf

The cat was done with one stroke of the brush. The stroke begins at the upper left corner and runs a clearly traceable course right to the end of the cat's tail. But how can a stroke begin in dense black ink, change to light grey, and gradually turn to black again? The answer is ink play: the artist manipulates brush, ink and water in the dipping, turning, in other words, in the 'writing' process.

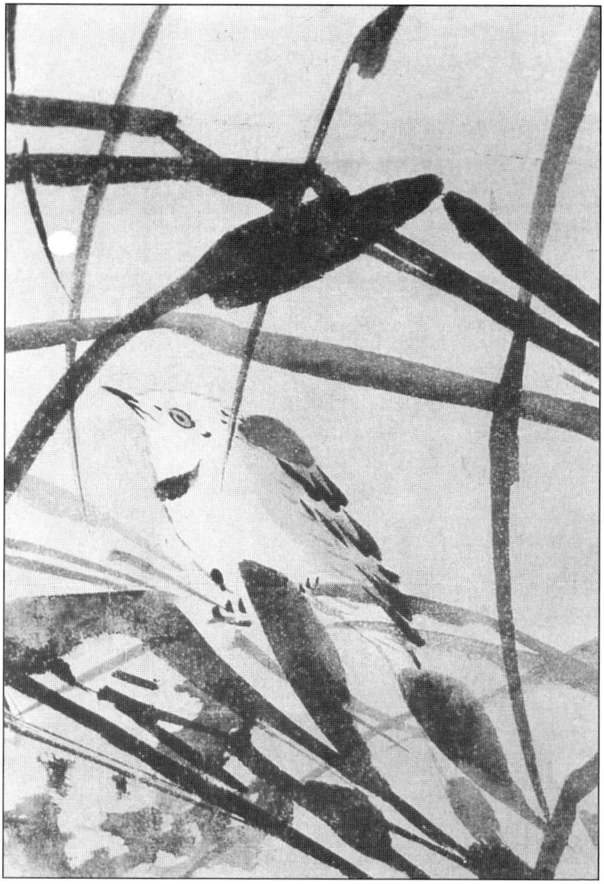

Bird Amongst Leaves detail
From a handscroll entitled *Birds and Trees*
By Lin Liang (1436–87), court painter.

A specialist in the 'flower-and-bird' genre of painting, Lin's art as a water-and-ink painter has been described as transcending realism and aspiring to the level of 'grass script' (a branch of calligraphy). Here one can see that every stroke in the picture is done with verve, consummate control and a seeming detachment—one of the ideals in the 'Tao' of painting implicit in the story of the *Book of Chuang Tzu*.

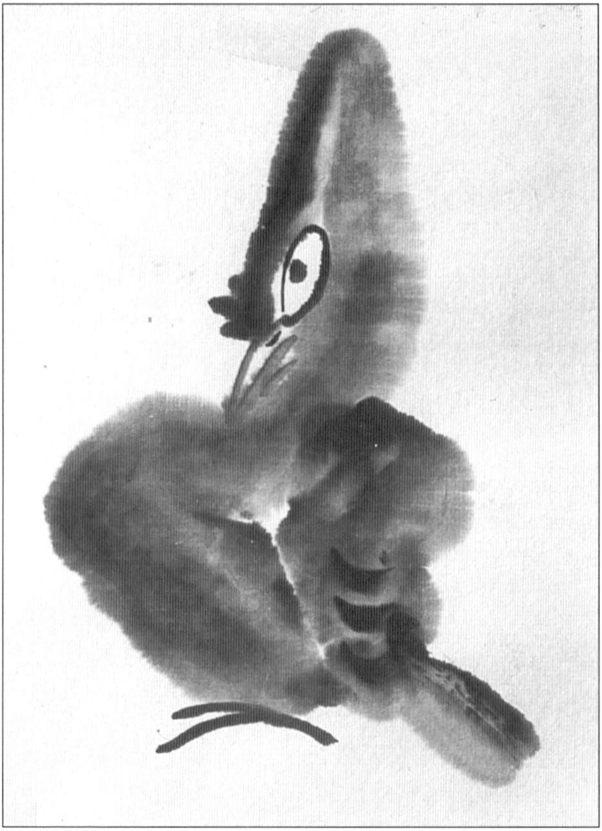

Bird
By Ding Yan Yung (1905–78)
Hanging scroll

This water-and-ink painting shows great command of the brush. The interplay of water and ink on a very absorbent surface brings out the texture of the bird's feathers. Ding was an ardent admirer of Bada Shanjen (see below) and had studied the latter's brush technique. It should be noted that to paint in the manner of someone whom the painter admires is a perfectly acceptable practice in the Chinese tradition. However, the painter usually acknowledges it in the inscription, if there is one.

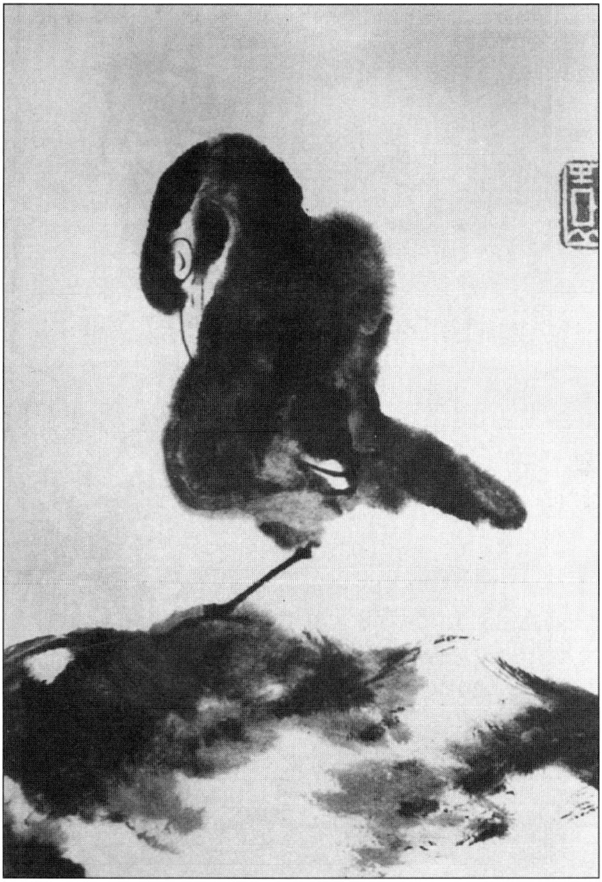

Bird
By Bada Shanjen (1625–1705), one of the 'Four Monks of Early Qing'
Album leaf

The style of painting in this picture—great economy of strokes and high expressiveness—is typical of Hsu Wei (1521–93). Bada's paintings, especially his birds and fishes, are characterized by their strangeness, a certain aloofness and defiance. His poetic inscriptions, whenever he includes them, are usually quite cryptic and unintelligible. In painting as well as calligraphy, Bada preferred the 'worn-out' brush.

8
The Creative Process

HAVING analysed the different techniques at the artist's command, it may come as a surprise to learn that the traditional Chinese painting (except perhaps portraiture) was not done with the painter facing the object or scene to be depicted; he did not in any obvious sense paint 'from life'. This does not mean that his painting had nothing to do with the supposed subject. It simply means that he was more concerned with 'capturing the spirit' of the thing than with a perfect reflection of its actual appearance. The relationship between verisimilitude and 'imaging the truth', discussed more fully in Chapter 2, is best exemplified by the sketches or rough outlines the painter makes for reference before the painting is begun.

Artists of many traditions use these sketches as groundwork for painting, but in Chinese art, special circumstances surround the way they are used. Before an artist ever learns to paint he knows the brush well and is able to handle it with ease. He has used a similar brush for calligraphy; the 'writing' of pictures will be an established habit. When the artist begins to paint, it is possible he will not be aware of this connection, but the alert viewer can immediately see that a Chinese painting is 'written': by tracing the stroke-sequence of a character or characters as one might read a piece of calligraphy, one can follow where an artist starts, how he carries on, and where he ends a painting.

There is a firm technical background to the preparation of a painting. An aspiring student practises the conventional type-forms that form the alphabet or vocabulary of Chinese art, just as he might practise cryptograms. And in both disciplines, a certain pedantic or learning-by-rote element is involved. His tutor, for example, may guide him with rules like the following:

> When planning to paint a landscape, first establish the 'host' and 'guest' positions of the mountains: then decide the configurations of the land. The brush must not be applied too heavily; otherwise, the result will be blurred and muddy. Neither should the brush pressure be too light, or else the result will be dry and without lustre. High hills should have their waists hidden by clouds: when several hills are envisioned, be sure they are not uniform in height. Mountain paths should be alternately seen and hidden by trees, rocks or other objects. Leaves should be grouped with discretion: some dense, some sparse.

A great painter of course will go beyond these conventional guidelines, and be ready to 'bare the chest', to be inspired in whatever circumstances. When the poet and calligrapher, Su Shih, once attended a literary gathering, a sudden impulse caused him to take up a brush soaked in red ink in order to paint some bamboos. His friends were surprised, ironically asking him, 'Where on earth do you find red bamboos?' To which he replied, 'Where on earth do you find black bamboos?'

Only an artist who has fully conquered his techniques can successfully improvise. Practised artists considered inspiration and wide experience of equal value to a thorough grounding in the technical process. Since these artists were often scholars, it was thought important that a painter both read and travel widely. 'Having read over ten thousand books, and travelled ten thousand miles, one can put pen to paper with such facility and ingenuity as if inspired' became a common saying, and Shih Tao confirmed this when he declared, 'Having seen to my heart's content all the hills and peaks, I can begin to make rough drafts and sketches.'

The idea of experience contributing to the state of emotional readiness of a painter is revealed in Su Shih's discussion with Wen Tung on how to paint bamboos. Wen Tung said:

> One can never capture the spirit of bamboo if one has to refer to the object constantly for details in the process of painting. The result can only be a lifeless plant. One must aim at grasping the whole bamboo, the finished bamboo, in one's mind, and then paint it in one breath. Only then can one get a good result.

When considering the manuals and type-forms of Chinese painting, it is easy to forget that individual techniques were intended to capture the spirit, or the 'truth' of nature. 'To have a complete bamboo in the chest' became an aesthetic expression to imply not only a well thought-out plan for the composition, but also an imaginative acquaintance with the material. In other words, technical prowess is nothing without a certain creative readiness. Such readiness derives from a high level of contemplation.

The apparent simplicity of the creative process, as shown by the great masters, meant that an inspired composition could appear on canvas in a very short period of time. However, a master of the brush, for example, Kuo Ju-Hsu's father awaiting his 'important guest', did not start until he had a complete vision of the planned picture before his mind's eye. The concepts that had matured in his mind for a considerable period of time depended on the moment of inspiration. Then, when all was prepared, the painter made a few apparently casual strokes, 'bared his chest'—and the work was done.

The moment the brush touches the paper for the first time is of great importance to the painter. Everything depends on the success of that stroke. Before he actually begins, when the brush is poised in his hand, the artist will inevitably feel there is nothing as hostile as the blank sheet in front of him. However, as soon as the initial stroke is achieved, the act of painting changes from a source of apprehension to one of intense joy.

Let us look here at the way the late Ding Yan Yung 'wrote' a painting, in this case a landscape. The following sequence of pictures formed part of a painting session; the painting or 'writing' itself required no correcting, and was done in only ten minutes. Unfortunately, very few modern artists have retained this skill.

Ding Yan Yung painting
This sequence of pictures was taken with the painter standing on the right. The first picture shows the brush going right, completing the first stroke. From there, every stroke can be followed and accounted for, showing the painter's great skill in achieving economy of brushwork without sacrificing artistic integrity.

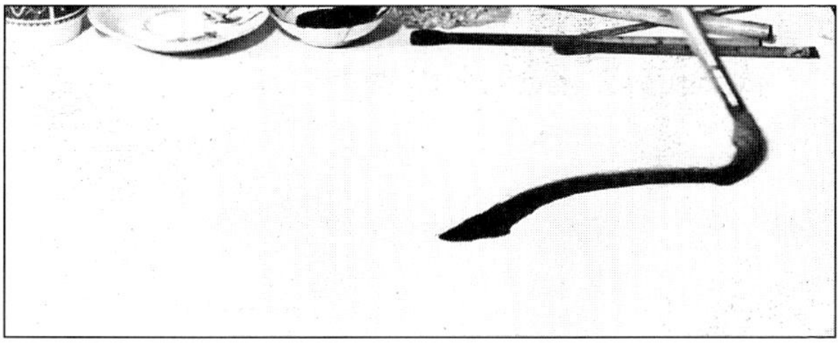

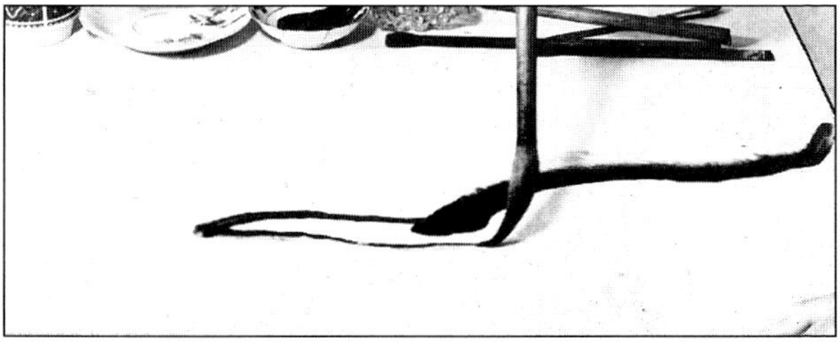

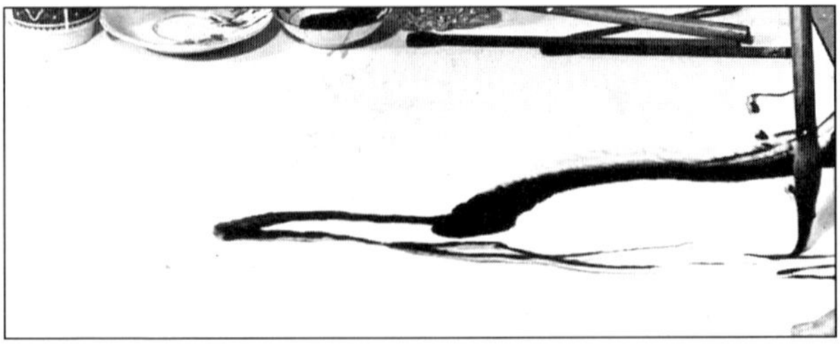

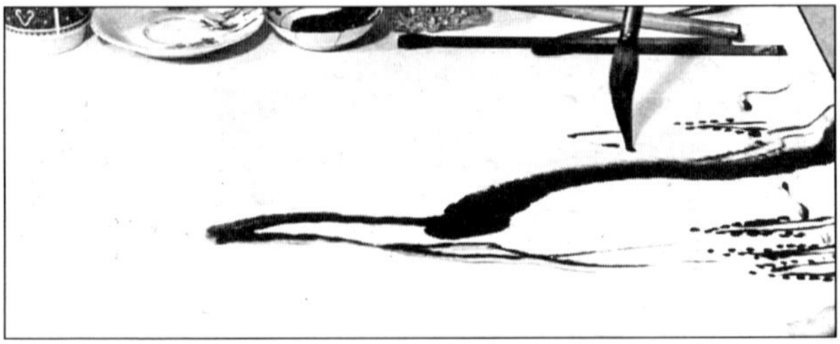

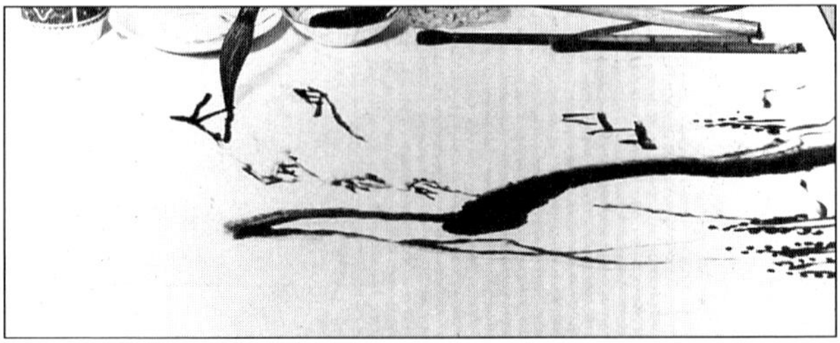

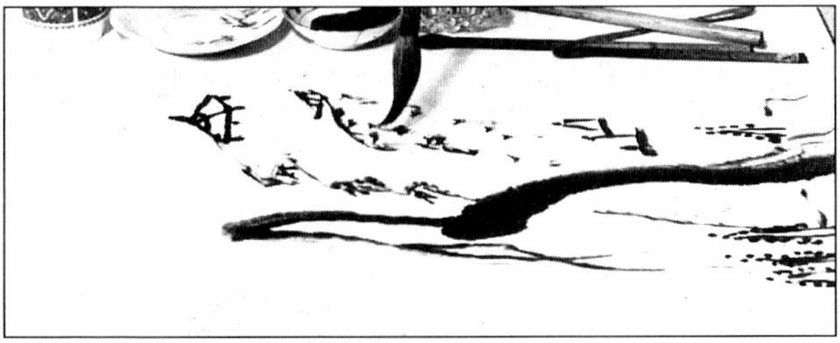

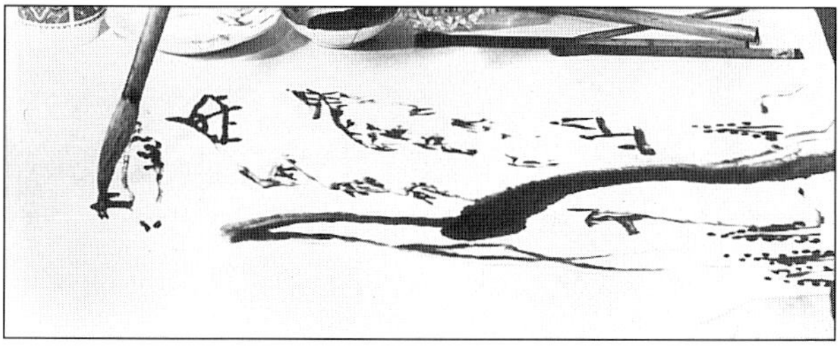

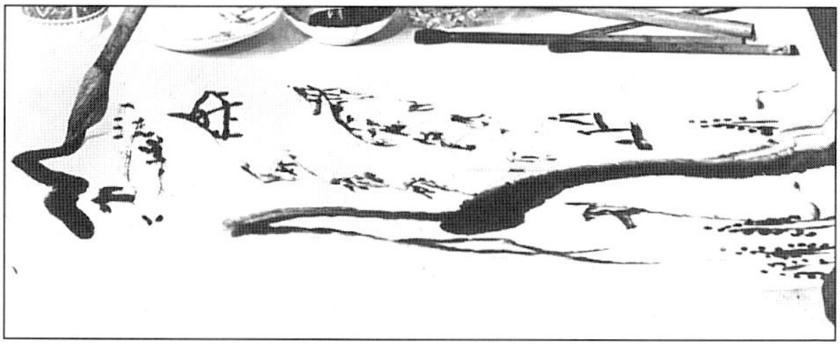

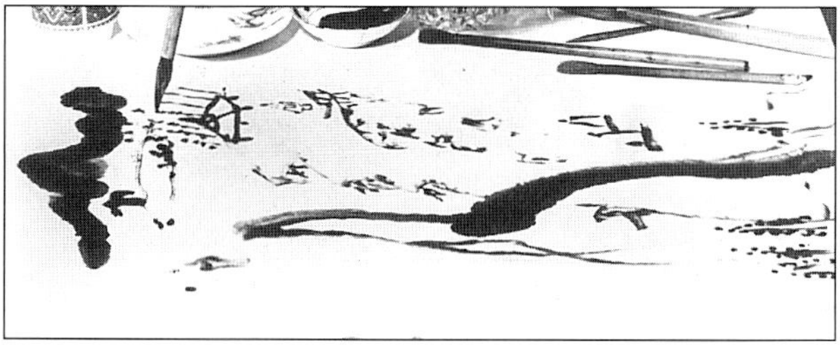

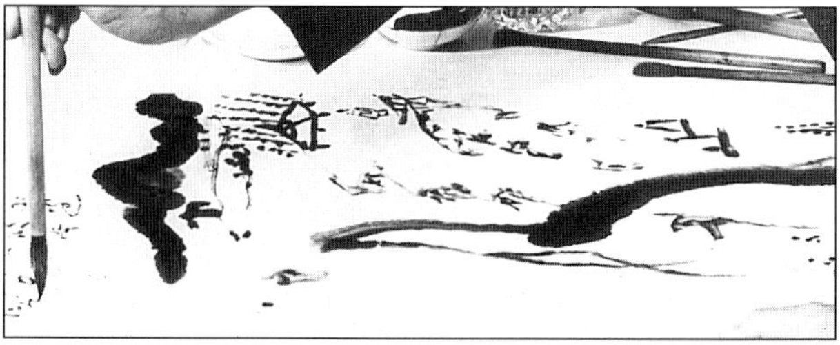

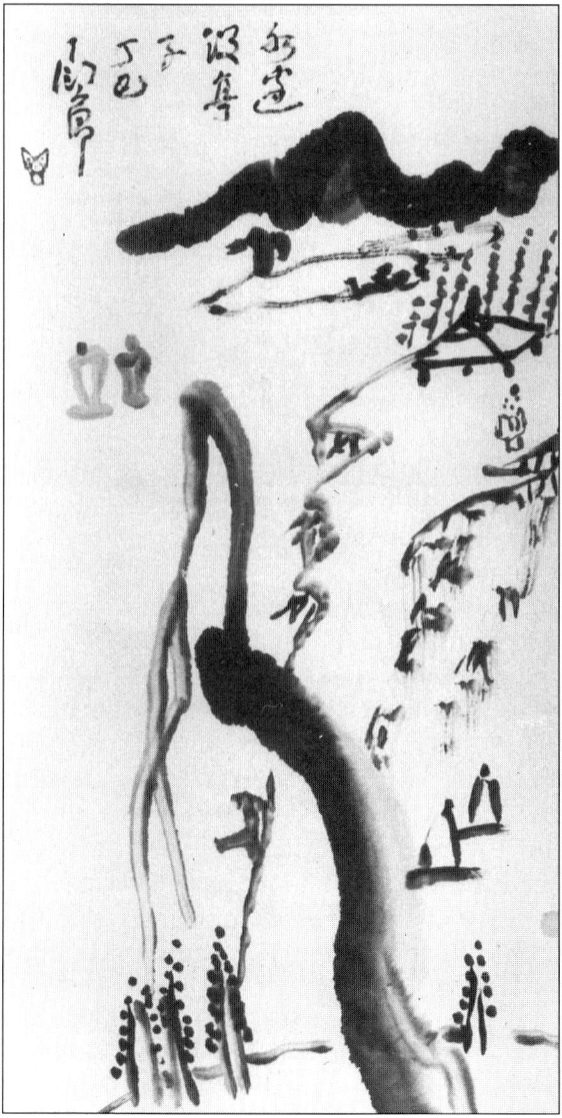

Din Yan Yung. The completed picture.

9

Looking at Paintings

THE previous chapters have aimed to present a general view of the art of painting, landscape painting being given priority on account of its special place in the history of Chinese art. Of necessity, these chapters have been highly condensed. The work of living artists has been excluded, mainly because modern Chinese painters have incorporated Western elements into their art, including instruments and materials as well as methods and ideas, and therefore any discussion of their work would involve a wide-ranging analysis of a rather different set of aesethetic values. Such a subject requires a book of its own. Instead of extending the argument to modern times, this chapter attempts to give an overview of the history of Chinese painting and to highlight some points of interest that have not been previously explored.

There was a lapse of six centuries from the earliest surviving examples of what may truly be described as 'painting' (on two fragments of silk), to the highly sophisticated painting called *Admonitions of the Imperial Instructress* by Ku Kai Chih (AD 345–418), a copy of which is now in the British Museum. Because of the perishable nature of the material, mainly silk, on which it was done, little has survived from the intervening period to indicate how painting developed.

From the fifth to the tenth century AD, there are a number of paintings attributed to names such as Li Szu-shun (AD 651–716), Wang Wei (AD 698–759), and Wu Tao Tzu (c. AD 675–716), but most of these claims cannot be substantiated and it seems that the paintings are copies made centuries later.

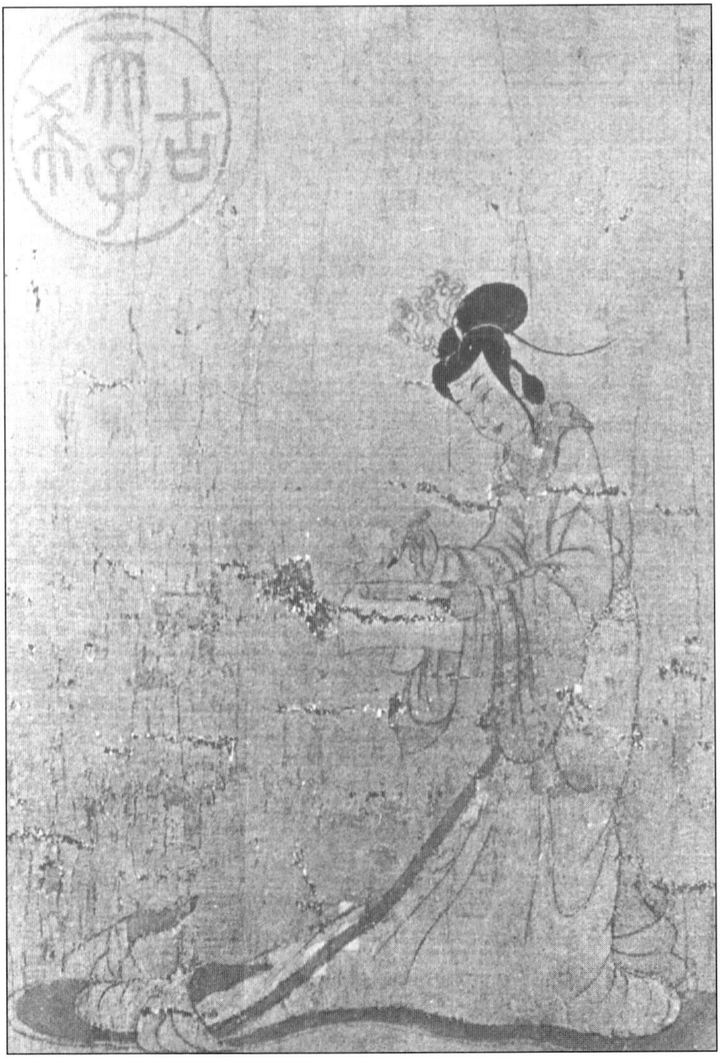

The Imperial Instructress, as she pens her *'Admonitions'* on the proper conduct for ladies.
By Ku Kai Chih (345–418)

From the fourth century AD until the Five Dynasties period (AD 907–960), the Dunhuang Caves in Gansu Province, with their frescoes mainly of Buddhist subjects, provide the only clear glimpses of Chinese art. However, in the ninth and tenth centuries AD, Ching Hao and Kuan Tung established landscape painting as a genre, along with Tung Yuan (AD 907–960) and Chu Jan (tenth century).

A leading painter of the Song Dynasty was Chao Chih, better known as the Emperor Hui Tsung (1082–1135), connoisseur and patron of the arts. He was an excellent calligrapher, who originated his own style of calligraphy called 'thin-gold'. Another original artist of the time was Mi Fei (1051–1107), best known for a calligraphic style characterized by eccentricity, which was reflected in a life-style that caused him to be nicknamed 'Mi the Mad'. A series of *ts'un* strokes in landscape painting—'Mi-dots'—was also named after him, consisting of dots of varying sizes mixed with dappled ink tones.

In the Yuan Dynasty (1206–1301), the art of painting was cultivated by such as Chien Hsuan (c.1235–1368) and Chao Meng-fu (1254–1322), but the best-known painters were the 'Four Yuan Masters': Wang Kung Wang (1269–1355), Wang Meng (1309–85), Ni Tsan (1301–74), and Wu Chen (1280–1354). Wang Kung Wang's landscapes represent the hills and valleys south of the Yangtze River, and his popular hemp-fibre strokes match the gentle and undulating terrain of the area. On the other hand, Wang Meng liked to capture the luxuriance and mellow fullness of the region by a skilful use of closely-knit clusters of strokes called ox-hair, which are now associated with him. Ni Tsan, whose serene but austere landscapes have won him special admiration, delighted in using a dry or 'thirsty' brush, 'treasuring ink like gold'. Wu Chen is best remembered for his paintings of fishermen framed in misty solitude, an embodiment of contentment in adverse circumstances.

During the Ming Dynasty (1368–1644), 'literati' painting became fashionable and continued to prosper. This genre has a predominantly literary flavour, characterized by allusions to antiquity and the pursuit of excellent brushwork for its own sake, rather than for its ability to precisely render reality. The work of Tai Chin (1388–1462), born near the beginning of the Ming Dynasty, took on some of the essential qualities of Song and Yuan Dynasty painting. Shen Chou (1426–1509), probably the best known of the Ming painters, was for a while tutor to Wen Cheng Ming (1470–1550) and Tang Yin (1470–1523), both of whom attained a fame equal to Shen's. All three had similar aspirations in their art—to emulate the masters of the past by assimiliating their techniques and scholarship.

In the sixteenth century, Sun Lung (dates uncertain) was much less widely known, but his expert use of the boneless technique still deserves special attention. A more well-known and equally important artist of the Ming Dynasty was Tung Chi Chang, who was famous both as a painter and as a calligrapher. He wielded immense influence over the artists of the early part of the Qing Dynasty.

The Qing period (1644–1711) was a very colourful one. Apart from the 'Four Wangs', who prided themsleves on being faithful disciples of the past, there were innovators and rebels such as the 'Four Monks of Early Qing', the 'Eight Eccentrics of Yangzhou', the 'Eight Masters of Nanking', and some court painters of foreign origin. In landscape painting, the Four Wangs exerted great influence, their aim being to emulate the past, and their greatest asset being their extraordinary skill. One of them, Wang Hui, said that an ideal landscape painting should have the best of the brushwork and ink

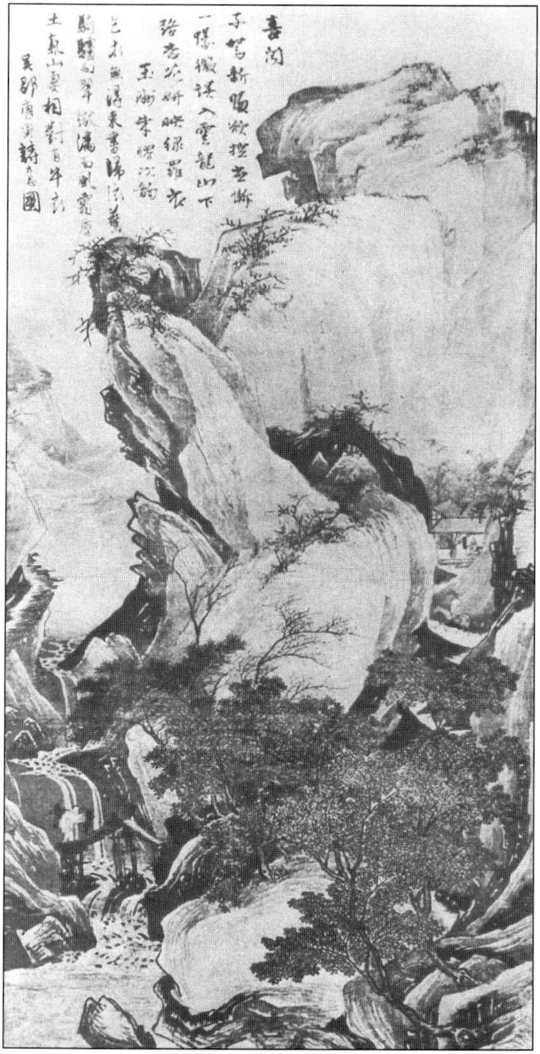

Going Home by Donkey
By Tang Yin (1470–1523).
Hanging scroll

tonality of the Yuan Dynasty, the grand schemes and emotional content of the Song Dynasty, and the rhythmic vitality of the Tang Dynasty.

Of the 'Eight Masters of Nanking', Kung Hsien (1618–89) particularly appealed because of his innovative use of *ts'un* strokes to create a sense of sombre majesty. Of the 'Four Monks of Early Qing', Bada Shanjen distinguished himself by an extreme economy of brush strokes, an unmistakable unconventionality, and a strong sense of defiance and aloofness. His contemporary, Shih Tao, demonstrated an amazing versatility in his use of textural strokes. The work of Hung Jen, also known as Chien Chiang, was reminiscent of Ni Tsan, except that he was bleaker and more severe in the organisation of his brush lines. Kun Tsan, on other hand, provides a stark contrast to Hung Jen, both in artistic temperament and treatment of the brush.

The most technically proficient of the 'Eight Eccentrics of Yangzhou' was Hua Yen (1682–1762), who started out as an artisan painting pictures on porcelain for one of the kilns in Ching Teh County, long famous as the porcelain capital of China. His influence on later painters of flowers and birds has been considerable. Bian Shou Min has never been surpassed in the painting of wild ducks. Every autumn he watched wild ducks amongst tall reeds on the marshes near his home, noting their movements and habits, which he then recorded in accurate and vibrant brush strokes.

One of the most colourful of the 'Eight Eccentrics' was Cheng Hsieh (1693–1765). After relinquishing a government post at an early age, he depended entirely on painting for his livelihood. His specialities are bamboo and orchid.

Giuseppe Castiglione (1688–1766), an Italian missionary and court painter, was well known for his efforts to combine Western realism with Chinese conventions and techniques.

He had various followers during his lifetime. Jan Po Nien was a leader of the Shanghai school and enjoyed extraordinary popularity during his lifetime, and for many years after.

Chi Pai Shih (1862–1957), perhaps the painter best known to Westerners, was specially remembered as a self-taught artist, starting life as a cowherd, then working as a carpenter and woodcarver, before achieving international fame late in his life.

The work of several of these artists and of all the periods in Chinese painting history is shown in the colour plates in this book, along with short notes on selected examples.

Further Reading

Bush, S., and Shih Hsio-yen, *Early Chinese Texts on Painting* (Harvard, 1983)

Cahill, James, *Chinese Painting* (Skira, 1977)

Ecke, Tseng Yu-ho, *Chinese Calligraphy* (Boston, 1971)

Fong, Wen C., et al, *Images of the Mind* (The Art Museum, Princeton, 1984)

Kwo, Da Wei, *Chinese Brushwork* (Allanheld & Schram, Monclair, 1981)

Goepper, Roger, *The Essence of Chinese Painting* (London, 1963)

Lai, T.C., *Brushwork in Chinese Landscape Painting* (Swindon, Hongkong, 1983)

— *Understanding Chinese Painting* (Schocken Books, New York, 1986)

Lee, Sherman E., *Chinese Landscape Painting* (New York, 1962)

— *The Colors of Ink* (Arno Press, New York, 1976)

Li, Chu-tsing, *Trends in Modern Chinese Painting* (Artibus Asiae, 1979)

— *Artists and Patrons* (University of Washington Press, 1975)

Loehr, Max, *The Great Painters of China* (Harper and Row, New York, 1980)

Siren, Oswald, *Chinese Painting: Leading Masters and Principles* (Lund Humphries, London, 1958)

— *A History of Late Chinese Painting* (Hacker, New York, 1978)

Sullivan, Michael, *The Birth of Landscape Painting in China* (University of California Press, 1962)

Van Gulik, R.H., *Chinese Pictorial Art* (Hacker, New York, 1981)

Index